31 girl

WHITAKER
HOUSE

deepercalling

31 GIRL

ISBN-10: 0-88368-808-5
ISBN-13: 978-0-88368-808-3
Printed in the United States of America
Australia: © 2002 by Mary Simpson
United States of America: © 2005 by Mary Simpson

Artwork & Design by Belinda McCullough, Bam Graphic Design. Photography by Amanda Spurling except: Photographs on pages 12 & 228 by Gaylene Trethewey; used on cover. Photograph on back flap by Gaylene Trethewey. Photographs on pages 61, 133, & 151 by Belinda McCullough.

W
WHITAKER
HOUSE

1030 Hunt Valley Circle
New Kensington, PA 15068
www.whitakerhouse.com

31 Girl Ministries
e-mail: marys@ccc.org.au

Library of Congress Cataloging-in-Publication Data

Simpson, Mary 1970–
31 girl / Mary Simpson.
  p.   cm.
Summary: "A coming-of-age book that shows girls in their teens and early twenties how to develop the good qualities and godly characteristics of the woman in Proverbs 31"—Provided by publisher.
Includes bibliographical references.
ISBN-13: 978-0-88368-808-3 (trade pbk. : alk. paper)
ISBN-10: 0-88368-808-5 (trade pbk. : alk. paper)
1. Teenage girls—Religious life. 2. Christian teenagers—Religious life. 3. Bible. O.T. Proverbs XXXI—Criticism, interpretation, etc. I. Title: Thirty-one girl. II. Title.
  BV4551.3.S565 2005
  248.8'33—dc22   2005001638

1 2 3 4 5 6 7 8 9 10 11   **W**   11 10 09 08 07 06 05

Especially for Jakey

(my little Lemuel)

I love waking up every day and seeing
your gorgeous smiling face. I am so blessed
to be your mom and pray that, one day,
you too find the 31 girl of your dreams.

Contents

foreword by
phil & heather baker

With three little girls growing up very fast, we are always on the lookout for excellent resources to help them in their walk with God. We've also asked God for wisdom on how to inspire and encourage them to put on the heart of the Proverbs 31 woman and to become virtuous, godly girls.

Mary Simpson has written what we believe to be a book that is at the forefront of a new revolution. A revolution that champions girls to become who God designed them to be, not what the world pressures them to become.

Now, to be able to put a book into their hands that encompasses all that we have wanted to teach our girls is an answer not only to our prayers but also tho those of any parents who are raising daughters.

The mixture of poetry, stories, practical tips, and theology makes this book unusual and unique and fills a much-needed gap in the material that is already out on this topic. It's written to the ones God intended this information to reach: our young girls.

Mary herself is an excellent role model as wife and mother, but more importantly, she is a fantastic pastor and a woman of great virtue and dignity. She is also the creator, designer, and dreamer behind the girlzLIVE online magazine, which now goes out around the globe.

To the sparkling, precious girls who share their stories within these pages, we applaud you. Your stories will have a far-reaching impact on a new generation coming up beneath you, all across this world. God will take your life stories and use them for good in many other lives, saving others from the pain or confusion that you once felt. We are proud of you all and thrilled God has planted you in our house. Your presence in God's house makes it increasingly richer, like a diamond with many facets, continuing to sparkle.

Thank you, Mary, for writing this book. It will make being a parent in the 21st century a little easier to navigate. But more importantly, it will help our beautiful, precious girls to become all that God has destined them to be—to shine, to be dazzling, to have fun, to care for others, to put their hands to their God-breathed purpose for being, to be ambassadors and role models in this world.

Our love to you.

Phil and Heather Baker
SENIOR MINISTERS, RIVERVIEW CHURCH

thank-yous

My darling husband, **Wayne**—I love you and feel immensely blessed to be your wife. Thank you for your love, support, encouragement, and constant faith in me. You cause me to simply blossom!

My **parents**—I love you both and am so grateful that you raised me up to be a godly girl! Thank you for your unconditional love and showing me how to be generous, caring, and down-to-earth.

My senior pastors, **Phil and Heather Baker**—thank you for believing in me, cheering me on, and entrusting me to speak into the lives of our priceless young people.

Mark and Penny Webb—a huge thanks for making this book possible and for your mentorship, leadership, and genuine care for me.

Aly and Marcus Passauer—I cannot express how precious you guys are to me, and I thank you from the bottom of my heart for your unwavering friendship and loyalty. You are a heaven-sent blessing to myself and Wayne, and I love doing life with you both.

My dear friend **Amanda Spurling**—thank you for your commitment to our young people (you embody the word "faithful") and for the time you spent in taking the most gorgeously stunning photos of our beautiful girls. You made them shine!

To the **31 Girls**—thank you for your honesty, vulnerability, and openness in sharing your stories. Each of you is truly remarkable, and I love how you have faithfully planted yourselves in our awesome church. May you flourish in every area of your life.

Riverview Youth & Young Adults Ministry—thank you to the staff, leaders, volunteers, and young people of our ministry. You are making an incredible difference and have been set apart to be a "different" generation. Simply put, you are heaven's best!

A **good woman** is hard to find and **worth far more than diamonds**....She is clothed with **strength** and **dignity**; she can **laugh** at the days to come. She speaks with **wisdom**, and **faithful** instruction is on her tongue. She watches over the affairs of her household and does not eat the bread of idleness. Her children arise and call her **blessed**; her husband also, and he praises her: **"Many women do noble things, but you surpass them all."** Charm is deceptive, and beauty is fleeting; but **a woman who fears the LORD is to be praised**. Give her the reward she has earned, and let her works bring her praise at the city gate.

Proverbs 31:10 (MESSAGE)**, 25–31** (NIV)

story

introduction:
once upon a time

"'Oh, my prince!' she cried. 'I have waited so long for you.'"

SLEEPING BEAUTY (FOLKLORE ADAPTED BY WALT DISNEY)

As a child, I loved fairy tales and reading stories of whimsical wonder and far-fetched fantasy.

I would let my imagination take flight as I pictured the beautiful, helpless princess, the handsome, brave prince who would rescue her and, of course, the token wicked stepmother who tried to thwart their happiness.

I would spend hours reading these incredible tales and wishing that I too would someday be rescued from the awful curse of having to clean my room, do my homework, and be generally teased and tormented by two older brothers. I dreamed of the magical day when my handsome prince, driving a sleek red sports car with a sunroof and automatic windows, would rescue me and we'd live happily ever after in a magnificent, all-white mansion by the beach.

But as is the case with children, I grew up and my dream turned into the reality of knowing that fairy tales just aren't true.

There's no such thing as kissing a frog and seeing it morph into a charming prince. I know firsthand because I was scammed into this so-called phenomenon and ended up bitterly disappointed when the frog simply hopped away. (Actually, I think it was pretty disgusted at having some girl try to smooch it.) But there is simply no such thing as enchanted forests, talking mirrors, cross-dressing wolves, and brick-laying pigs!

There is, however, one thing about fairy tales that is true.

It's the phrase "and they lived happily ever after." You see, although fairy tales may not be real, the Bible definitely is, and it is filled with stories of characters who were eternally blessed by the favor of God—people who were literally chased for the rest of their lives by goodness and mercy!

And there are many "happily ever after" stories in the Bible that I love. But my all-time favorite is Proverbs 31. It's the description of a girl who is simply amazing.

When I first started reading about the 31 girl, I was in total awe. Here was a girl who had the "It" factor—she just seemed so perfect, ideal, and almost unbelievable. Her life literally had a fairy tale touch to it. But it soon became apparent she was no fantasy. A closer look at her life revealed she possessed qualities that I, as a young woman eager to please God, could develop and apply in my life.

My only regret is that I wish I had uncovered her treasury of qualities earlier in my life, so that I could have developed them in my teenage years, well before I became a wife and mother. And that is what this book is about. Rather than being a fairy tale, this book is a true story of the legendary qualities of the 31 girl.

Now I know some of you are already thinking, "I know this woman you're talking about. Isn't she some dull housewife who cooks, cleans, and does some sewing? I can't relate to her, and I'm getting bored just thinking about her." But stay with me on this because, believe me, you will be surprised how remarkable this girl is.

If you are a girl in your teens or twenties, then this book has been especially crafted, inspired, and written with you in mind. It's about how you can develop the qualities of the 31 girl in your life right now and know with confidence that you are priceless, precious, and prized by God.

Proverbs 31 is a treasure chest filled with priceless qualities that adorn the life of this very classy chick, and this book will bring her to life for you as you read the following chapters. Some of her qualities will challenge you and some will inspire you, but at the end of the day all of them are attainable.

Spread throughout the book are real-life tales from modern-day princesses. These are girls who are on the journey to becoming virtuous 31 girls, and I hope their stories will inspire and uplift you.

Also included at the end of each chapter is a "Treasure Tip." Each Treasure Tip is a sparkling gem that will relate to your spirit, soul, or body and can be used to further enrich your life.

So grab something scrumptious to eat, get comfy in your fave chair, and let's take a journey together in discovering the ultimate "It" girl of all time!

a good woman is hard to find and worth far more than diamonds. good woman is hard to find and worth far more than diamonds. good woman is hard to find and wor

July 31

chapter 1:

character is a girl's best friend

"And the moral of that is—Oh, 'tis love, that makes the world go round!"

ALICE'S ADVENTURES IN WONDERLAND (BY LEWIS CARROLL)

Proverbs 31:10

"A good woman is hard to find and worth far more than diamonds." (MESSAGE)

Have you ever had a crush on someone?

I developed my first full-blown crush before I was even a teenager. The unknowing recipient of my love and affection was absolutely gorgeous. I could gaze at him for hours and not grow tired. In fact, that's literally what I did! His name was Indiana Jones, and I was introduced to him in the film *Raiders of the Lost Ark*.

We met again through the sequels, *The Temple of Doom* and *The Last Crusade,* but, as is the case with most first-time crushes, my fickle heart had already moved on and my interest had waned.

But seriously, I loved watching all the Indiana Jones movies. They were jam-packed with action, excitement, fun, and, of course, romance. Indiana was always on the hunt for rare artifacts and riches. He tirelessly searched for ancient objects and treasures that were simply priceless.

And this is how our girl of the moment is described.

Proverbs 31:10 tells us that finding a good woman is pretty hard. And if she is found, then she is worth much more than mere diamonds, rubies, or any other precious gem. In other words, she is an exquisite and invaluable treasure. Put simply, she is priceless!

When something is priceless, that means it is irreplaceable, unique, and usually rare. And what makes the 31 girl rare is the fact that she is a girl of virtuous character. Today in our world of corruption, deceit, lies, and bankrupt morals, good character is hard to find. It is an exceptionally rare trait.

But what exactly is character? What does good character look like?

D. L. Moody said, *"Character is who you are when no one is looking."* It's the real you, the private you. Who you are without the mask or charade. Character is not developed overnight. It takes diligence and commitment. In fact, in my life, I will forever be on a quest to develop my character to be more Christlike.

So what makes up good character? Well, I've read many books on character development. However, for me, I believe the Bible is the perfect reference point.

Galatians 5:22–23 says, *"But the fruit of the Spirit is love, joy, peace, patience, kindness, goodness, faithfulness, gentleness and self-control."*

These nine fruits of the Spirit are the qualities that I believe we need to develop in our lives if we want to be known as young women of character. And although they are all important, the number one quality of good character is LOVE.

The Bible says that even if we could perform miracles, understand all mysteries, and give all our money away to the poor, if we don't have love operating in our lives, then it means nothing. Absolutely ZILCH! Put simply, the greatest quality of all is love.

So how do we develop this foundational character quality of love in our lives? Well, I'm glad you asked. I believe there are three main ways:

1. Stay Close to Love
The Bible says in 1 John 4:8 that God is love. This means that by staying close and plugged into the ultimate Source of love, we cannot help but be changed. As you spend quality time with God daily, His character is deposited into you. The more time you spend with Him, the more you become like Him.

Staying close to God also keeps us "in love" with Him. Revelation 2:4 says that we should not forsake our first love. Above all else, our heavenly Father must be our first love. That's not to say that we can't have other loves in our life, but He has to be our priority, our personal Number One.

2. Act in Love

Put love into action. First John 3:18 says, *"Let us not love with words or tongue but with actions and in truth."* It's not enough just to think or speak it; we also have to put love into practice. Now you may be thinking, "Hey, that's not so bad; I can tell my parents or friends that I love them. I can be good, kind, and patient with them. It's cool. I've got this love thing covered."

But this is where love gets difficult because the Bible says in Matthew 5:44–48, *"Love your enemies....If you love those who love you, what reward will you get?...And if you greet only your brothers, what are you doing more than others? Do not even pagans do that? Be perfect, therefore, as your heavenly Father is perfect."*

We need to love those who annoy us, who are unkind and rude to us. Those who backstab, betray, and belittle us. We also need to love those whom we and others consider to be "unlovable."

Jesus said that it's easy to love those who are good to us, but the truth is that anybody can do that. The real test of character is to love those few people in our lives who really rub us the wrong way. This means irritating brothers and sisters, friends who have hurt us, and those who have abused our trust. We need to love them and pray for them.

Now I know that for some of you this is going to be a real challenge because there are people in your life who have seriously hurt you. They've mistreated you, whether emotionally, physically, sexually, or mentally. But this is where God comes in, because there is no way in the world that we could love these types of people without His help. And that brings me to my third point.

3. Ask God for Help

Too often we rely on our own strength, talent, and ingenuity in life. But if we want to be young women of character, then we need to ask God for His help. Acting in love toward those we dislike and despise is absolutely impossible without God's help. We need to ask Him every day to help us walk in love toward others.

Romans 5:5 says that God has poured out His love into our hearts by the Holy Spirit. This is an important Scripture to remember when we find that loving others is too hard. Remember that He has already deposited His great, all-consuming, and forgiving love into us, and by His help we can draw upon it and love those who are "too hard" to love.

Love so **amazing**, so **divine**, demands my soul, my life, my all. (ISAAC WATTS)

Adele's Story

I was born in New Zealand and come from a broken home. My mother is in her third marriage, and I have nine siblings to various parents.

My dad was a country cop and often brought home his frustrations from work. He always had to be in control and never said that he loved us or was proud of us. In fact, he didn't know how to show us any affection.

Dad wanted his family to be perfect and was a firm believer in the Scripture "spare the rod and you'll spoil the child." So he overdisciplined us, usually with the cane, resulting in blood blisters. We were also hit until we stopped crying. Therefore, I learned to clam up and hold in my emotions.

One day when I was about ten, my mom met another man and they grew close. He promised to be her "knight in shining armor." Mom fell for his charm and told Dad she was leaving and taking the children. Dad exploded and threatened her with his gun but eventually calmed down and let her go. I cried as I waved good-bye because even though he wasn't a good father, he was still my dad.

Soon after that, my stepdad's personality changed, and he became abusive to us. He would punch my younger brother in the head, verbally abuse us, and kill my pet cats to punish me. When my mom and stepdad had a baby boy, he was abusive to him too. I tried protecting him but couldn't do anything, so eventually I gave up. When I reached thirteen, my self-esteem was so low that I thought of killing myself. I felt ugly and worthless, and I hated being me.

One day during one of the times when Mom and my stepdad were separated, my mom met a man and started getting close to him. When my stepdad found out, he was furious and broke into the house. My mom locked herself in her bedroom, but he bashed open the door. To stop him from hurting her, I ran in and pushed him out of the way so she could escape, but he grabbed me by the throat, pinned me to the wall, and repeatedly punched me in the chest. Mom screamed at him to stop, and then he grabbed Mom and took off in the car. He threatened to kill her, because if he couldn't have her, then no one else could either. I called the police, and they arrested him and took him to jail. He stayed in jail for three months but was let out because Mom dropped the charges and took him back. I didn't speak to her for a long time because I was so angry, but I knew it wasn't going to help, so I simply accepted it.

Due to my abusive experiences I didn't know how to show my feelings. I put up a wall around my heart so I didn't have to deal with any more pain or rejection. Eventually God helped me overcome these insecurities and brought me to a place in my heart that I had never surrendered to Him—allowing Him to be my Father. I dearly loved God, but because my earthly fathers had hurt and damaged me deeply, I had a problem letting God be my Father.

I also had to learn to forgive the people who had hurt and abused me. I found it extremely hard to forgive, but I knew I had to let go of the past or else I would become a victim of it. One night at youth group someone prayed for me and said that I couldn't let go and forgive in my own strength, so God would give me His strength and grace to help me love and forgive, and I did.

The things that hold us back from growing in God and blossoming into the people He intended us to be are bitterness, hatred, and unforgiveness. By storing these inside, they eat away at our core and critically affect us. Not everyone is served with a wonderful life, but you can change it for the better, and you don't have to be a victim of your circumstances.

I believe that by making a commitment to stay close to God, putting love into action, and asking Him to help us love others, we can develop this quality of love in our lives. And by having love operating in our lives, we are journeying on the path to becoming girls of godly character.

Let's Pray

Father,
I pray that You would strengthen me with power through Your Spirit in my inner being, so that Jesus Christ may dwell in my heart through faith. I pray that I, being established and grounded in love, may be able to comprehend with all the saints in heaven what is the width and length and depth and height of the love of Christ. I pray that I may also know this love that is incomprehensible so that I can be filled to overflowing with the fullness of God. (Based on Ephesians 3:16–19.)

treasure tip
Hang Out with God

By spending daily quiet time with God, we not only allow Him to speak into us but also to transform, shape, and craft us into the unique and pure girls He wants us to be. A consistent daily quiet time is a habit we need to form in our lives. Regular time with God rejuvenates, energizes, and soothes us. It's not something that should be rushed or that we feel obliged to do. Spending time with God should be a joy, not a chore. So every day, look forward to your time with God as precious and important.

There are many ways to have a quiet time, and this is only one of them.

What you need to get started:
- A notebook
- A pen
- A Bible (one that you can easily understand; a youth study Bible is good)
- A favorite worship CD or tape

Commit to a time and place:
- Morning, afternoon, or evening...whatever works best for you. Aim for the time when you are the most awake and energetic. (Remember, we need to give God our best, and that includes the time when we are at our best.)
- There are no set rules on how much time you need to spend, but you do need to make time with God a priority in your life.

Now what?
- Put a worship CD or tape on and allow your heart to focus on God.
- Read a passage from Psalms or Proverbs, and from the Old and New Testaments.
- Pray to God.
- Write in your journal.

Remember, your daily quiet time doesn't need to be complicated. Simply spend time with God and allow Him to challenge, inspire, and speak to your heart through His Word.

brings him good, not harm, all the days of her life. Her husband has full confidence in her and lacks nothing of value. She brings him good, not harm, all the days of her life. Her husband has full confidence in her and lacks nothing of value. She brings him good, not harm, all the days of her life. Her husband has full confidence in her and lacks nothing of value. She brings him good, not harm, all the days of her life. Her husband has full confidence in her and lacks nothing of value. She brings him good, not harm, all the days of her life. Her husband has full confidence in her and lacks nothing of value. She brings him good, not harm, all the days of her life. Her husband has full confidence in her and lacks nothing of value. She brings him good, not harm, all the days of her life. Her husband has full confidence in her and lacks nothing of value. She brings him good, not harm, all the days of her life. Her husband has full confidence in her and lacks nothing of value. She brings him good, not harm, all the days of her life. Her husband has full confidence in her and lacks nothing of value. She brings him good, not harm, all the days of her life. Her husband has full confidence in her and lacks nothing of value. She brings him good, not harm, all the days of her life. Her husband has full confidence in her and lacks nothing of value. She brings him good, not harm, all the days of her life. Her husband has full confidence in her and lacks nothing of value. She brings him good, not harm, all the days of her life. Her husband has full confidence in her and lacks nothing of value. She brings him good, not harm, all the days of her life. Her husband has full confidence

chapter 2:
all for one and one for all

"There was a kind of rushing noise, and a long chord played along with it. All round the churchyard there were hundreds of old friends. They rose over the church wall all together."

THE ONCE AND FUTURE KING (BY T. H. WHITE)

Take **my life**, and let it be **consecrated**, Lord, to thee.
(FRANCES RIDLEY HAVERGAL)

Proverbs 31:11-12

"Her husband has full confidence in her and lacks nothing of value. She brings him good, not harm, all the days of her life."

In today's world, you only have to flip through the paper or watch the news to be bowled over by stories of snollygosters, illywhackers, and hornswogglers.

"What?!" I hear you exclaim.

Don't stress, they're not accounts of attempted alien abductions or mutant, marauding Muppets.

Snollygosters, illywhackers, and hornswogglers are cheats, liars, and deceivers; they are the con artists, professional tricksters, and rip-off merchants. Unprincipled individuals that you couldn't, wouldn't, and shouldn't trust.

We're taught as we grow up that we shouldn't trust strangers, the used car salesman, or the local politician. We're taught that trust really needs to be earned, and we need to be very careful whom we give our trust to because some people will use and abuse us.

Sadly, it seems as though trustworthiness and loyalty are in short supply. However, our 31 girl has cultivated a beautiful quality in her life.

Proverbs 31:11-12 says that her husband has full confidence in her, and she brings him good and not harm. This Scripture means that she is dependable, reliable, steady, trustworthy, truthful, and loyal—a girl of integrity. Her husband doesn't have any need to worry because he knows that he can totally trust her; she's not going to betray him. To sum it up, she is faithful!

So how do we cultivate and produce faithfulness in our lives? Well, it's as simple as making a commitment to do it.

There's no formula or ten-step program; you simply have to make a firm and unwavering commitment to be a faithful person. Make a commitment to be someone who will be loyal, trustworthy, and honest regardless of how hard it is or in spite of the consequences.

If you make a decision now to develop a habit of faithfulness in your life then it will naturally be grafted into your character. You see, your character is a result of the habits in your life, and furthermore your destiny is dependent upon your character. So if you want your destiny to be exciting and God-inspired, then your character needs to be made up of godly habits.

Let's take a look at some areas you can be faithful in:

Time
We all have time. Time is something that God gives all of us in equal measure, no matter what our abilities are. Ecclesiastes 9:11 says, *"Time and chance happen to them all."* How faithful are you with your time? Are you using your time well or are you squandering it? I've heard many girls complain that they just don't have enough time, but the truth is that they are just not using their time well or they cram too many unproductive activities into their days. We've got to make a decision (sometimes a tough one) to eliminate the activities that waste and whittle away our time.

Be faithful with the time God has given you. Time is a commodity that can never be stored away and used later on. How you spend your given time is really up to you. After today is gone, it's gone forever. Use it wisely.

Other People's Stuff
If you want your own things, you must be faithful in looking after other people's things. You need to start by being faithful with things that don't even belong to you. I'm sure you know what it feels like to loan a friend an item of clothing only to have it returned in worse condition, so be faithful with other people's belongings.

It's also important to be faithful with information that people give you. If someone tells you something in confidence, you need to honor that person's trust and not divulge the information. Even if you are bursting at the seams to tell someone, don't! Be self-controlled and trustworthy with other people's private matters.

Luke 16:12 says, *"And if you have not been trustworthy with someone else's property, who will give you property of your own?"* If you are faithful with what belongs to other people, then you can be sure that God will bless you with your dreams and desires.

God

Many times we can be fickle, and our passion for God can become lukewarm. Staying on fire for God requires us to be faithful in our habit of daily spending quality time with Him. Being faithful means putting aside how you *feel* at the time and just doing it. Many times you're not going to *feel* passionate for God, you're not going to *feel* like worshipping, and you're not going to *feel* like spending time with Him. But if you are serious about developing your character, then you can't be driven by what feels good at the time. Make a decision to be passionately faithful to God and stick to it regardless of your feelings.

real life

Amanda's Story

I first toddled into our church in December 1980. My mom was invited to church by her good friend Mandy, who had been talking to her about God. This alone I continually thank God for. My mom has said she doesn't want to imagine what our lives would be like if she hadn't been invited to church and accepted Christ as her Lord.

During these times, I watched my parents serve diligently in whatever area they could. They have set an example of faithful and joyful service that I followed. I have been blessed with great parents to model, but if you haven't, know that your children will have awesome Christian parents that they will praise God for.

My early teenage years were spent having crushes on guys, talking about guys, crying over guys, wondering what guys thought, and doing my hair fifty times to be noticed by guys. I got to sweet sixteen, never been kissed, and said hello to dating. But allow me to give you some advice. The qualities in God's girls, like yourself, are so irresistible to guys, and it breaks my heart to see awesome Christian girls dating guys who don't have the same godly stuff on the inside. The lessons I learned are too many to write here, but let me say that you can pray all you want for him to turn to God, you can stay firm that you won't give yourself to him before marriage...but no matter how gorgeous he is, how funny or popular, or how much he says he loves you...IT IS NOT GOD'S HIGHEST AND BEST FOR YOUR LIFE.

In January 1995 I was at youth summer camp and decided to make a commitment to God to seek His plan for my life, to be faithful to Him, and not to compromise by dating someone He had not chosen for me. It really is an incredible ride when you get on God's path for your life.

April 1996 was a turbulent time for me and many others. The youth pastor at the time left, and so did most of the other youth leaders. It was a time of total chaos. Many of these people were my good friends and leaders. I was considering what I should do when, one night at youth group, a thirteen-year old girl asked me if I was going to leave too. I looked at the faces of the four girls waiting for my response, and God broke my heart for them. I told them they could trust me, and I would stay. That young girl went on to be a leader in our youth ministry!

Another big thing I want to tell you about is SEASONS in our lives. It is important to know about being steadfastly faithful with the little and big things. And sometimes one door will open or one will close, which is all in God's plan. A door was miraculously opened for me to be part of Youth With A Mission (YWAM) for the second half of 1998 in Colorado, USA.

I got to preach to about two hundred people in an open-air theater in Monterrey, Mexico. We built a drainage system for two days for the Hopi Indians on their reservation in New Mexico. I worked in orphanages and sang and preached at a men's prison in Albuquerque. We helped build a church, and the pastor was so thankful that he killed his cow, and we ate that all week...all of it! On day four, I asked him if I could have some of his rice cereal...but he insisted I must eat the cow, so I ate some more intestines!

My first day of YWAM, I was chatting to God and told Him it would be great if I could see snow before I left. On my last day, I walked over to the chapel to reflect on everything God had done in my life. As I was praying, tiny snowflakes started falling, and I screamed with excitement (actually I think I cried), because God is so faithful with all things, even the littlest desires of our hearts. After my time with YWAM, I returned to Australia and started serving again in our youth ministry.

Perhaps you have a very different story; just know how important it is to be faithful wherever you are. I look forward to bigger adventures that require more faith and trust in God—because I know He has our lives in His hands and is so faithful!

I hope that you've been challenged to get serious in the area of faithfulness. Let's make a commitment to be faithful girls of God—trustworthy, reliable, and loyal. A generation of girls who are known for their integrity-founded characters—girls who take after their heavenly Father, the Holy One who is steadfast, never changing, and amazingly faithful to us.

Let's Pray

Father,
I thank You that Your Word says that I can be confident that You will faithfully finish the work You began in me. I pray, Lord, that I too develop this quality of faithfulness in my life. Help me to be a girl of integrity, someone who is known for her honesty, trustworthiness, and loyalty. Lord, I want to be like You.

treasure tip
Memorial Day

Now is the perfect time to remember how faithful God has been in your life and to start living a lifestyle of gratitude.

First, get yourself a quality notebook, which will serve as a Gratitude Journal. Start to write down and remember what God has done in your life. If you've only just recently become a Christian, then you can start by thanking Him for His amazing saving grace and for eternal life.

Many times we go through life, taking God's blessings and His faithfulness for granted. A Gratitude Journal forces us to put aside for a few moments the busyness, turmoil, or trying times of our lives and pour out our hearts in uncontainable thanks to our magnificent God. It's also humbling to look back in a year's time and read how faithful God has been to you. So allow every day to be a Memorial Day for God.

Write down and count your blessings...lest you forget.

She selects wool and flax and works with eager hands. She selects wool and flax and works with eager hands.

Priscilla

31

chapter 3:
a lesson from
the seven dwarfs

"Now that I'm here, perhaps I'll tidy up a bit."

SNOW WHITE AND THE SEVEN DWARFS
(FOLKLORE ADAPTED BY WALT DISNEY)

Proverbs 31:13

"She selects wool and flax and works with eager hands."

Have you ever had a song in your head that was insanely annoying? It was like an irritating broken-down record (sorry, make that a CD) that kept repeating itself, over and over and over again, driving you totally crazy.

Well, I had one of those in my head the other day, and it went something like this...

"Heigh-Ho! Heigh-Ho! It's off to work we go! We keep on singing all day long with a Heigh! Heigh-Ho!"

Yes, that's right, it was that Top 10 hit on the fairy tale charts by the original boy band—the Seven Dwarfs. It was spinning around and around in my head, and all I could think of was those cheesy guys and the perennially perky Snow White grooving away in the background.

I never really figured out whether these guys worked for some international diamond conglomerate or were self-employed, but they were definitely into searching for precious gems. And they obviously loved and looked forward to their work because every morning they sang that catchy little number as they left their comfortable communal cottage. And as I pondered their poetic ditty, I started thinking that there's a lesson in that for all of us. Work is not something that should be loathed, avoided, or even dreaded.

Proverbs 31:13 clearly states that the 31 girl selects wool and flax and works eagerly. Now, that doesn't mean that you have to go out and get yourself some taffeta and chiffon and be chirpy about it, but it does mean that you need to apply diligence to whatever you put your hand to.

You see, the key ingredient for success in anything that you decide to do, whether it be school, a sport, or volunteering at church, is hard work.

The 31 girl has a great heart attitude toward work: "She willingly works with her hands." She gets into her work diligently and cheerfully. She literally "puts her hands joyfully to work."

Many times we view work (chores, serving, homework, etc.) as something that we're forced to do. But the girl who is priceless and beautiful in God's eyes throws herself wholeheartedly into her work. She lives out the Scripture in Ecclesiastes 9:10: *"Whatever your hand finds to do, do it with all your might."* In other words, don't just halfheartedly do your chores, finish your homework, work at your job, or serve at church; do these things with zesty gusto. Put your heart into it; do them ecstatically, passionately, and willingly.

Now I know some of you are probably rolling your eyes and thinking, "How am I supposed to feel cheerful about doing chores around the house or my history essay or serving burgers to rude customers at McDonald's?" Well, hopefully the following tips will help you in your quest to be more like the 31 girl:

Tip 1: Work for God
Colossians 3:23–24 says, *"Whatever you do, work at it with all your heart, as working for the Lord, not for men, since you know that you will receive an inheritance from the Lord as a reward. It is the Lord Christ you are serving."*

There are times when your boss is really going to annoy you. Times when you can't be bothered with showing up at youth group to help on the set-up team. Times (and I know this one is really rare) when your parents will bug you about tidying up your room or your roommates will go off at you about cleaning up around the house. But it's times like these when you need to remember that it's actually God you're working for, and not people. He is your reason for what you do. When you lose perspective, get back on track by remembering that you're serving Jesus.

Tip 2: Be Positive

Every day you have a choice to look for either the good or the bad in things. So decide now to look for the benefits and be positive. Instead of moaning and groaning about work and chores, look for the benefits. Smile at those grumpy customers at work because you may be the only one who smiles at them all day. Clean your room, and you'll probably find that missing sweater you've been looking for all winter. You may not see any benefits in having to study history at school, but when you tackle your homework or assignments, be positive about it. If anything, at least you've learned something new and, who knows, one day you may have to remember that obscure war date when you're a contestant on *Who Wants to Be a Millionaire!*

Tip 3: Value Each God-Given Day

Psalm 118:24 says, *"This is the day that the LORD has made; let us rejoice and be glad in it."* Sometimes, in the everyday chores and duties of life, we can lose the buzz of awakening to a new day. The 31 girl eagerly gets into her work one day at time and one task at a time. How you live each day is your choice; choose to live your days striving toward excellence and becoming more like your Father. He will use this day (if you allow Him) to fashion you into the girl He has destined you to be.

real life
Bridget's Story

I grew up in a strong Christian family in a small farming town in New Zealand. There are five kids in my family, and I'm the second oldest.

Growing up in a big family with three younger brothers meant there was always a lot of work to be done, so from about the age of ten I was regularly helping my mom with chores around the house such as washing, feeding, and bathing the baby of the family and helping to prepare meals.

Financially, life was difficult for Mom and Dad, and they often struggled to make ends meet. Dad was a shearer and often had to travel away for weeks, sometimes months at a time, in order to work. My mom really relied on my help during those times.

When I was thirteen, my parents made the hard decision to leave New Zealand and move to Corrigin in Western Australia. Dad had consistent work there, and it meant that our family didn't have to be apart any more.

I finished tenth grade at Corrigin District High School and then went to boarding school for two years in Narrogin. I was quite a motivated student and achieved good grades in all my subjects. After finishing my final year, I moved to Perth, rented a small apartment with my sister (who was also studying), and started a commerce degree at college.

During the next three to four years, I was fairly inconsistent in living the Christian life. I was unsure of myself and my faith and often felt torn between what I'd been taught in my Christian upbringing and what my friends were doing. A lot of my friends were people from the country who were into partying pretty hard, and their motto was "go hard or go home." Because I wasn't very sure of myself, sometimes I would go hard and other times I would go home! I wasn't sure where I fit in or where I wanted to fit in. I wasn't fully comfortable with what my friends were doing, but I held back from being fully involved in church.

I enjoyed the pace of life at college—I was always busy with study, my casual job, or my social life. I worked hard to get good grades, and at the end of my three-year degree in marketing and public relations, I applied and was accepted to do honors. The next twelve months were even more fast-paced as it was an intense year of assignments and research, combined with the fact that my social life was at an all-time high as I hung out with my fellow honors students.

After I finished my honors project and left college, life quieted down for me a lot. My sister moved out to the country to start her first job, and a lot of my college friends dispersed and went traveling. I suddenly found myself quite alone and looking for a full-time job.

Emotionally I was at the lowest point in my life, because after studying so hard for so long, I couldn't find a full-time job in my area of study even though I desperately tried. After months of rejections and working in temporary secretarial jobs, I became quite discouraged. At the same time, I had become very conscious of the wrong things I had done and came to the realization that the only way to rid myself of the anxiety I felt was to get right with God again.

One night at home I asked Jesus to come back into my heart. I asked for forgiveness, and I declared to Him the way I would live my life from then on. That night I made my faith absolute, and I haven't looked back since.

It was many more months before I found a full-time job in public relations. That was a real character-building, faith-developing time for me as I learned to put my trust in God and surrender the plans and dreams I had for my life to Him. God brought me to the point where I could honestly say to Him, "God, if this is Your will for my life, working as a secretary, I will do it."

Once I prayed that prayer to God, the doors opened for me immediately, and within a week I was working in a full-time public relations job—the type of job I had always wanted. I ended up working for that company for two years before coming on staff in the youth ministry at Riverview Church.

I have learned that in order to "get ahead" in life, whether at school, college, or in the work force, I don't need to push and maneuver my way around, impressing people in order to get noticed. As I diligently applied myself, the rewards came.

I'm very grateful to my parents for instilling in me the ethic that when you do a job, you do it properly. By applying that principle, I've always had opportunities before me. Life is most exciting and adventurous when you're fully connected to God and part of a vibrant local church. I really encourage you to make the decision to remain connected to God and planted at church despite what may be happening around you—because there you will find peace, joy, and hope that you'll never experience out in the world!

I hope those tips have helped you gain a new perspective toward work and being diligent. It's also important to remind ourselves that the girl we're reading about in Proverbs did not just instantly appear all perfect and perky. She developed these qualities over a period of years when she was young, well before she became a wife and mother.

God has put this girl in the Bible as an achievable ideal for us to aspire toward. So together, as girls who love God, let's develop her amazing qualities in our lives and become a generation of 31 girls.

Let's Pray

prayer

Father,
I pray that whatever work my hands do, I will do it eagerly, energetically, and with excellence. I want to live my life serving, honoring, and pleasing You. Lord, this is the day that You have made, and I look forward with expectation to what this day holds. This day is a gift from You, and today I give my gifts back to You.

treasure tip
Hands Up

With all the work your hands will eagerly be getting into, I think it would be a good idea to spoil them. Here are ten steps to a great manicure.

1. Remove any nail polish on your nails.

2. Soak nails in a bowl of warm water for a few minutes.

3. Use an orange stick (cuticle stick) to push back your cuticles.

4. Use the nail file to clean under your nails.

5. Use the emery board to file your nails. (Never use a metal nail file, as it is too harsh for your nails.) Don't file back and forth; instead, go in one direction toward the tip of the nail. File toward a nice oval shape.

6. Massage in a hand lotion all over your hands and nails.

7. Wipe away lotion from the top of your nails.

8. Paint a thin layer of base coat on each nail and allow to dry.

9. Use the color of your choice and paint a sheer coat on your nails. Allow to dry and paint another coat.

10. When the polish has dried, put a layer of top coat over your nails.

Quick tip:
If you ever have dry, cracked hands, lather them in sorbolene cream, rich hand cream, or olive oil. Put on a pair of rubber or fabric gloves, leave them on your hands for twenty to thirty minutes (or even overnight). Remove and rinse. Repeat every three days until you begin to see an improvement in your skin. This tip is guaranteed to leave your hands as soft as a baby's bottom.

ne merchant ships, bringing her food from afar. She is like t
chant ships, bringing her food from afar. She is like the merch
s, bringing her food from afar. She is like the merchant shi
ing her food from afar. She is like the merchant ships, bring
ood from afar. She is like the merchant ships, bringing her fo
afar. She is like the merchant ships, bringing her food from a
is like the merchant ships, bringing her food from afar. She
ne merchant ships, bringing her food from afar. She is like t
hant ships, bringing her food from afar. She is like the merch
s, bringing her food from afar. She is like the merchant shi
ing her food from afar. She is like the merchant ships, bring
ood from afar. She is like the merchant ships, bringing her fo
afar. She is like the merchant ships, bringing her food from a
is like the merchant ships, bringing her food from afar. She
ne merchant ships, bringing her food from afar. She is like t
hant ships, bringing her food from afar. She is like the merch
s, bringing her food from afar. She is like the merchant shi
ing her food from afar. She is like the merchant ships, bring
ood from afar. She is like the merchant ships, bringing her fo
afar. She is like the merchant ships, bringing her food from af
s like the merchant ships, bringing her food from afar. She
ne merchant ships, bringing her food from afar. She is like t
hant ships, bringing her food from afar. She is like the merch
, bringing her food from afar. She is like the merchant ship
ng her food from afar. She is like the merchant ships, bringi
ood from afar. She is like the merchant ships, bringing her fo
afar. She is like the merchant ships, bringing her food from af

Bread

chapter 4:
the "cherry-on-top" attitude

"Pat-a-cake, pat-a-cake, baker's man,
Bake me a cake as fast as you can.
Pat it and roll it
and mark it with a T,
And put it in the oven for Tommy
and me."

THE CLASSIC MOTHER GOOSE (EDITED BY ARMAND EISEN)

Proverbs 31:14
"She is like the merchant ships, bringing her food from afar."

I LOVE shopping!

Let's face it, if you're a human being of the XX chromosome type, then the browsing, window-shopping, and buying gene has been embedded in your DNA. And these days, when you want a shopping fix, all you need to do is go to one of the suburban department stores and take your pick from the smorgasbord of retail goodies.

But in ancient times, there were no such things as department stores. In fact, the closest thing to a department store were the merchant ships, which would travel long months to deliver their precious and exclusive goods to keen buyers. They traded spices, precious jewels, clothes, and beautiful pottery. Many times they encountered rough seas, treacherous pirates, and enormous challenges, but they still sailed on. The wait was definitely worth it for those waiting to satisfy their shopping fix. It's to one of these merchant ships the 31 girl is compared.

Now, I've heard of guys who are "built like a Mac Truck," but being compared to a huge cargo ship is one compliment that most girls would want to steer clear of. But this verse brings out another awesome quality of the 31 girl that God wants us to develop.

She's the type of girl that goes the extra mile or miles for others. In fact, she puts in that extra bit of effort that makes all the difference. I like to call it the "cherry-on-top" attitude.

A chocolate cake with all the yummy icing on top looks great, but when you add that bright red cherry, it just about makes it perfect. And that is the attitude our 31 girl has. She's not content with just doing what is expected of her, she puts in that 10 percent more that makes a 100 percent difference. She is a second-miler!

Jesus said in Matthew 5:41, *"If someone forces you to go one mile, go with him two miles."* This Scripture is about having a generous "extra-mile" attitude, which in every circumstance will go beyond what is expected to encourage and help out.

However, the 31 girl is not the only one in the Bible with a cherry-on-top attitude. In fact, the Bible is chock-full of second-milers to inspire us, and I think the person who really sums it up is the poor widow who literally gave all she had (Mark 12:41–44). Here was a woman who had practically nothing to give yet still gave her all. She was definitely a second-miler in giving. But she was also a woman of faith. She knew that she would never lose by giving to God. When you give Him a teaspoon, He gives you back shovel loads of blessings.

God went the extra mile for us by sending His Son Jesus Christ to die for our sins. We didn't deserve it, yet He loved us so much He was compelled to do it. Since we are daughters of the Most High King and made in His image, we too should feel compelled to go the second mile in our lives.

A great place to start is in the area of encouragement. Many times when someone has done something great, we forget to tell them. But encouragement is empty when it's left on the inside of us. We need to give our encouragement away because everyone needs encouragement. Author Derek Bingham describes encouragement as the "oxygen of the soul" and says hundreds of people end their lives every year because of a lack of it.[1] So let's go the extra mile in encouraging those around us—not in a cheesy, fake way but with sincerity.

The next time you think about the difference someone has made in your life, don't just think about it; write them a letter, e-mail them, or send them a card.

When someone's name pops into your head and you're wondering how they're doing, stop wondering and pray for them or give them a call. Tell them you're thinking about them. Believe me, not only will they probably be surprised, but they'll also be grateful. There is not a single person alive who hates encouragement. We all thrive on it and need it.

Most importantly, be generous in your encouragement. Don't ration it out or be stingy with it. When someone's done something good or said something great or worked hard, TELL THEM, TELL THEM, TELL THEM! Put that cherry on top by being an excessive encourager. No one can despair from too much encouragement but people can certainly despair from a lack of it.

A girl who I am blessed to know and who has literally gone the extra mile is Jessica. Jessica is an intern with our youth ministry from America. She has paid to come over to Australia and serve in our youth ministry for a year, joining our school outreach program, Powerhouse Roadshow (a multimedia presentation of life skills). In the following pages, you can read her story.

It takes so little to make us sad,
Just a slighting word or a doubting sneer,
Just a scornful smile on some lips held dear;
And our footsteps lag, though the goal seemed near,
And we lose the courage and hope we had—
So little it takes to make us sad.

It takes so little to make us glad,
Just a cheering clasp of a friendly hand,
Just a word from one who can understand;
And we finish the task we long had planned,
And we lose the doubt and the fear we had—
So little it takes to make us glad.
(IDA GOLDSMITH MORRIS)

real life

Jessica's Story

I was raised in a small town in Michigan. Both my parents are Christians, as well as my younger sister.

Though we went to church as a family, the small town we were in was "spiritually dry" and bent on tradition rather than the heart of God, and we soon fell away from the church. As a result, my relationship with God withered, and when I reached high school, I really began to suffer without Christ.

At thirteen, I was consumed with image and looks, and as a result, I developed the eating disorder anorexia. It was the loneliest, most heartbreaking time in my life. I hit rock bottom at seventy pounds with a heartbeat of forty-four beats per minute. I was near death.

After months of suffering, a friend's mother stepped in and took me to a group therapy session, where I was desperate to overcome my problem. Though I began to get better, the experience had left a deep wound in my heart, and I began to search desperately for acceptance, purpose, and love.

Soon after, I developed the eating disorder bulimia, where one binges on food and then forcibly vomits it up. This was a problem that I kept as a dark secret, because all I could feel was immense shame. I also started drinking excessively, and this became entertaining to me. I loved being drunk, and alcohol soon played a major part in my life. I can say without hesitation that at age fourteen, I was an alcoholic—drinking by myself and taking from my parents. I soon began to smoke pot and again found myself at rock bottom when I snorted the stimulant drug called speed. Life was nothing to me, and I had an incredible apathy toward myself, others, and family.

When I was fifteen, my family moved to California. It was a culture shock for me, yet I continued to do the same self-serving things I had done before. My first friends were three atheist girls who, over time, caused me to begin doubting my faith. However, my parents never gave up on me and we began to go to Horizon Church in San Diego, California, where God started to knock on the door of my heart once more. It was astonishing to me to see "life" in church. It wasn't long before God really began to intervene in my life, and I started attending Daybreak Church youth group.

God started to knock down the walls in my heart and open my eyes to Him. I stopped hanging out with my atheist friends and rededicated my life to Jesus. Over time God has broken me, cleansed me, repaired and healed me, and then built me up. I joined the staff at Daybreak Church and am blessed beyond imagination at, not only His transforming power, but how He has used every one of those experiences in my life to help and counsel young women and other students.

Jesus Christ is truly my Savior, my Redeemer, and everything in between.

Be conscious of going the extra mile. God wants us to take after the 31 girl who, like the merchant ships, went out of her way to do good and bring good to others.

Doing that little bit extra and going out of our way for others can sometimes be a challenge. However, we would do well to remember the words of A. Lou Vickery: *"Four short words sum up what has lifted most successful individuals above the crowd: a little bit more. They did all that was expected of them and a little bit more."*

Let's Pray

Father,
I thank You that You went the extra mile by sending your Son Jesus Christ so that I could become Your daughter. Lord, I pray that every day I will become more like You. Help me to go the extra mile by giving generously of myself to You and to those around me. I want to be a second-miler and Your vessel of encouragement.

treasure tip
E-Day

Remember back to the last time someone really encouraged you. It could have been through words, or maybe you received a card or letter that just blew you away. As good as it made you feel, I bet the person who gave you the encouragement felt even better!

An E-Day is all about giving encouragement, and not only will it make you feel fab, but it will also be uplifting and life-giving to someone else.

Here's what you'll need to get started:

- Writing paper or cards plus envelopes. Even better, why not make your own cards and decorate them individually?

- The names and addresses of at least five special people who have really made an impact on your life by either their friendship or their leadership.

- A good pen (remember, you're going to be doing lots of writing, so it needs to last and be comfortable to write with).

- Time to sit down and really write something special that you know will encourage the people you have chosen to write to.

- A favorite Scripture or quote to include in your letter or card.

- Stamps to mail the letters or cards. I know it's easier these days to send an e-mail, but writing letters and mailing them just makes the encouragement that extra bit special. Also, it shows the person who receives the letter or card the time and effort you took to do it.

An E-Day is all about taking time out of our rushed lives to acknowledge the difference others have made to us and to generously lavish them with encouragement.

31 girl

chapter 5:
the "d" word

"Little Boy Blue, come blow your horn,
The sheep's in the meadow,
the cow's in the corn.
But where is the little boy who looks after
the sheep?
He's under the haystack fast asleep.
Will you wake him? No, not I,
For if I do, he's sure to cry."

THE CLASSIC MOTHER GOOSE (EDITED BY ARMAND EISEN)

Proverbs 31:15

"She gets up while it is still dark; she provides food for her family and portions for her servant girls."

Have you ever played the game **Word Association?**

It's where someone says a word or name and then you say the first thing that pops into your head. Let me give you an example: **Apple**—(word association) *fruit, Granny Smith, healthy.* Another example: **Donald Trump**—(word association) *millionaire, "you're fired," weird hair.*

Now that you've got the hang of it, what are the first words that pop into your head when you think of **Discipline?** *Hard work* or *boring?* Maybe even *pain?* Although most of us associate negative words with the word *discipline,* it is actually a quality that God wants you to develop and one that can become a lifesaver for you.

Discipline means "to bring under control," and it's a quality that the 31 girl has developed in her life. She gets up while it's still dark outside, which means it's very early in the morning. She gets food ready for her family and work organized for her servants. She has control over her household but, more importantly, over herself.

Now don't get too stressed because this chapter is not about getting up early and making bacon and eggs for your family. It is, however, about gaining control over your life and the things that can get in the way of your walk with God. This chapter is about the necessity of disciplining yourself.

The ancient philosopher Plato said, *"The first and best victory is to conquer self."* Throughout your life, you will have many challenges and battles with relationships, school, work, and family, but the biggest challenge and battle you will have is with yourself.

And gaining control over yourself will undoubtedly be your greatest victory. You will never gain and sustain success in life without self-discipline.

One of the most important aspects in your life that you can gain control over and be disciplined in is your soul or emotional self. This is an area of your life that can make or break you. When you enter adolescence, your body goes through a roller coaster of changes, and these physical changes effect you emotionally. And to top it all off, when you're premenstrual, you can sometimes get moody, irritable, teary, angry, crabby, and happy—all in the space of an hour!

Let me say from the outset that there is nothing wrong with emotions. God gave you emotions so you could express yourself. However, you need to gain mastery of your soul and not let your emotions rule you.

To gain control in your emotional life, you need to develop soul-healthy habits. Your life is made up of a series of habits, which in turn form the foundation of your character. If you have developed soul-damaging habits in your life, then you need to break them and develop healthy ones to replace them. These negative habits fall into three main categories:

Soul-Destroying Habits

Jealousy, comparing yourself to others, and envy are habits that, if left unchecked, will be like parasites eating away at the core of your individuality. God made you distinctive and unique, and when you compare yourself to others or are envious of another person's life, then you are challenging God's handiwork—which is you. To destroy this habit you need to develop a "habit of thanksgiving." One of my all-time favorite quotes is by Condoleeza Rice. She said, *"It is a dangerous thing to ask why someone else has been given more. It is humbling—and indeed healthy—to ask why you have been given so much."* [2]

Develop a daily habit of thanking God for what you have. Start a Thanksgiving Journal, and every day write a prayer of thanks in it to God for what He has given you.

Believe me, by doing this, you will see that you have been abundantly blessed, and it will change the way you look at life. Those habits of jealousy and ungratefulness, which eat away at you, will eventually be eradicated by disciplining yourself to be grateful. Instead of finding it hard to be happy when those around you are successful, you will be able to celebrate with them.

Soul-Hardening Habits

Being unable to control your temper, holding grudges against other people, and being easily offended will only harden your soul. These habits will cause your heart to become calloused and impenetrable. God wants your heart to be soft and not heavily weighed down.

The best way to destroy this habit is to develop a "habit of delay." Seneca said, *"The greatest cure of anger is delay."* [3] Many of us have heard the advice of counting to ten to calm ourselves down. But I would go further by saying count to one hundred or one thousand if that's what it takes to calm down or gain some perspective. Pausing to question whether you will make a fool of yourself by your outburst is crucial in remaining softhearted. Get into the habit of understanding that many times it's just not healthy to get offended or steamed up about stuff. My advice is let it go and travel through life "lightly" by letting go of emotional baggage.

Soul-Weakening Habits

Nehemiah 8:10 says, *"For the joy of the LORD is your strength."* By habitually complaining and being pessimistic, you weaken your soul (and it doesn't help that you usually also look like you've been sucking on a lemon). But a joyful attitude in God will strengthen you. So instead of being a "killjoy," learn to develop a habit of being a "joyrider." Strengthen your soul by finding as many Scriptures on joy as you can and meditating on them. Memorize them so joy will flow out of your heart instead of negative, complaining comments. See yourself as a fountain of joy rather than a squirt of lemon juice.

I stand amazed at the lives of some of the girls in our youth ministry. Many of them have been through such difficult family situations and upbringings, yet they have decided to keep their souls sweet. This is Kate's story:

real life
Kate's Story

I'm not great at writing an eye-opening story about my life experience and the courage from God that has helped get me through each day of my life. However, I have a poem that I once wrote that explains who I am and what I have been through and the courage that I had to get through it.

Time has only the ability to heal what others can't.
Courage has only the ability to stand up for what others won't.
But she was new to a world that would fight her and make her bleed.
And bleed she did.
Normal is nothing she knew and this would begin to tear her down.
Death is nothing she wanted but it would be thrown upon her constantly.
Her mother mentally ill and suicidal, her father withdrew from the problems, and her sister didn't understand.
Sexual abuse would be her first of many painful things to come.
She did not remember her tragedy but was reminded of it daily.
Her cousin was now a threat to her family, but he was never threatened.
A string of death-related incidents would arise with her mother.
The girl was helpless and confused, and many times she would shut herself away from any problems.
It did not grow better for a family who were at constant war with each other but who still loved each other dearly.
Cancer would strike the ailing mother who was starting to improve her illness.
And the little girl who was once so young in the world now had to fight to keep herself alive in it.
So the battle continued and is still going and things aren't better nor are they worse.
But this girl has the courage to fight for life and hold on to it the best she can, 'cause it's the only way she knows how to live.

This is my story. It's not an average one, but it's mine, and for some reason, I wouldn't change it. I have the courage to stand up for the life I have because no matter what, life is my greatest gift of all. And that's the lesson I have learned so far.

O Lord, that lends me **life**,
Lend me a **heart**
replete with
thankfulness.
(WILLIAM SHAKESPEARE)

Girls, if you want your soul to be healthy, you have to take control and develop habits that will strengthen rather than destroy it. This will take time, and probably a lot of tears, but the results will far outweigh the effort.

H. Jackson Brown Jr. said, *"Talent without discipline is like an octopus on roller skates. There's plenty of movement, but you never know if it's going to be forward, backward, or sideways."*

If you want to go forward in life, your biggest challenge will be to discipline yourself. But you can do it by making a decision to develop soul-healthy habits and relying on God for His help.

Let's Pray

prayer

Father,
I thank You that You made me unique and distinctive. There is no one else in the world like me. I pray that every day You would help me gain control over my soul and those habits that damage it. Lord, I want to develop healthy habits in my life, which strengthen my soul and soften my heart. I put my life in Your hands and pray that You mold me into the young woman You desire me to be.

Re-create yourself

Throughout your life you will go through times (and for various reasons) when your spiritual, emotional, and physical gauges are low and you feel like you are "running on empty." And one of the simplest ways to ensure your emotional gauge doesn't get low is to engage in regular **recreational activity**.

Recreational activities keep our souls topped-off, and as a result we feel regenerated.

So here are some ideas that may help you feel full again:

- Walking along the beach
- Painting or drawing
- Reading an engrossing novel
- Playing music
- Singing or writing songs
- Hanging out with good friends
- Going to the movies
- Cooking
- Going for a bike ride
- Surfing, swimming, sailing, windsurfing
- Visiting the art museum
- Being creative by making your own stuff (e.g., clothes, cards, gifts, jewelery)

We're all different and unique, so what you love doing may not have even been mentioned, but it's important to recharge your batteries. So make sure that you do whatever "recreates you" at least once a week.

She considers a field and buys it; out of her earnings she plants a vineyard.

31 gifts

chapter 6:
money, money, money!

"The Owl and the Pussy-Cat went to sea
In a beautiful pea-green boat,
They took some honey,
and plenty of money,
Wrapped up in a five-pound note."

THE OWL AND THE PUSSY-CAT (BY EDWARD LEAR)

Proverbs 31:16

"She considers a field and buys it; out of her earnings she plants a vineyard."

At the time of writing this chapter, I was having a nice cup of tea and a scone at a riverside café (sounds very "granny-ish," doesn't it?).

This café has some of the best views of the beautiful city of Perth. It is located on the edge of the Swan River in South Perth and looks out to the skyscrapers and business buildings in the city.

As I sipped on my tea and savored every mouthful of my yummy scone topped with jam and whipped cream, I thought about all the busy people in those buildings, hurrying through their day, looking at ways to make money and ensure their businesses were successful. Some of them would succeed and others would fail. Some would get promoted and others would be told they no longer had a job. But all of them had one goal in mind: to make smart money choices. And, in a nutshell, that is what this chapter is about. To be money wise.

Our 31 girl is definitely not clueless when it comes to money. Verse 16 describes how she takes the opportunity to buy a piece of land, and then out of her profits she plants a vineyard. Now, let me make it very clear that I don't believe she woke up one morning and decided to get out her brown clay piggy bank (they didn't have pink plastic ones back then) and start wheeling and dealing in blocks of land. This girl learned how to be successful with money early on in her life.

She sowed wise investments and, as a consequence, reaped well-earned profits. When it comes to the matter of money, she is one sharp pencil! And my message is that you can be too. It's never too early or too late to start managing your money.

Regardless of whether you are in your teens or twenties, it's important that you develop wise money habits in your life. Being money wise will carry you in good stead throughout your life. It will enable you to fulfill your dreams (especially if money is needed to finance those dreams), be a blessing to others, and build God's house.

So let's not wait any longer. Here are two main points you can start with to become money wise:

Get a Plan in Place

There's no use going through life just wishing your dreams would come true. With anything in life you've got to have a plan in place to make them happen.

One of the best money plans I know is called the **10/10/80 Plan**. It's incredibly simple, but you need to be disciplined to make it successful. Basically you need to see whatever money you receive as a big pie.

Now you've got to get an imaginary knife and cut up that big pie into three slices. Two small, 10 percent size slices and one big, 80 percent size slice.

First slice: The first slice should be 10 percent of the money you receive. For example, if you receive $10 allowance a week, then 10 percent of $10 is $1. If you work and you get $100 a week, then 10 percent of $100 is $10. So far, so simple.

This first slice is called your "tithe," and it needs to go to God. One of the best habits I developed in my life from an early age was the habit of tithing. Tithing is giving 10 percent of whatever money you receive to God and into His house.

When you tithe, you are depositing money into your "spiritual bank account." But unlike banks on earth that charge you fees for looking after your money, God promises to open the gates of heaven so that His blessings will literally flood out upon your life. Give 10 percent to God and He gives you back more than you can contain. Sounds like a pretty good investment deal to me!

Second slice: The second slice of the pie is also 10 percent. But instead of giving this slice away, you need to save it. This means opening up a bank account and depositing your 10 percent slice or getting yourself a pink plastic piggy bank (they don't have brown clay ones anymore) and putting it away.

The main discipline here is that you train yourself to stick to a savings plan and not spend everything you earn.

By sowing a habit of saving you will reap the benefits of being able to one day purchase that funky denim jacket, your own car, start a business, travel overseas, or fulfill your dreams. Rather than being chained to the shackles of credit card debt, you remain liberated by paying cash out of your savings.

Remember, though, not to get discouraged by the "small" amount you may start with. That small amount will not remain small. It will grow if you remain focused and disciplined.

Last slice: The last slice of the pie is the biggest at 80 percent. If you receive $50 a week, then 10 percent goes to God ($5), 10 percent is saved (also $5) and 80 percent is left which amounts to $40. This last slice is yours to do with whatever you please. It can be spent on entertainment (going to the movies), beauty (new nail polish), food (chocolate, chocolate, and more chocolate), clothes (a new top), or bills (cell phone calls, rent/board). And if you don't need to spend it, then don't! Save it or give an offering to God, which is money over and above your tithe.

This is the slice that you need to be careful with. Many times people can spend more than they receive, which results in debt. This is not a healthy habit to develop, so it's important that you pay attention to what you are spending.

The key to remember is that if you don't have the cash to buy those new shoes, then don't be tempted to pay for it on plastic because not only will you pay for it later, but you'll pay for it with interest.

Be Frugal

A little while ago, our senior pastor at Riverview Church, Phil Baker, spoke about being frugal during one of his messages at church. I definitely learned a lot from it. Being frugal is not being stingy or cheap. Frugality is all about being careful and economical with your money. It means not being wasteful or allowing yourself to get shafted by some shop assistant.

Rather than spending $5 buying your lunch, make it instead and you'll save heaps. Go to the movies on a day when it's only half price. Plan to buy some of your clothes during sale time. Don't shop when you're in a bad mood because you'll be more likely to buy impulsively. Shop around and compare prices at different stores; why pay $10 for a T-shirt at one store when the same item will only cost you $7 at another store?

Be smart and work out ways to make your money go further. Frugality is an important habit to develop in our lives.

Being money wise is definitely a quality that God wants you to develop. Money is a resource that can help or hinder you in life, and it's your attitude toward it that determines that.

So put a plan in place today, learn to be frugal, and when an opportunity (that requires money) knocks on your door you'll be able to act on it like the 31 girl.

Janine's Story

When I look back over my twenty-two years of life, I can plainly see the workings of God's hand. Right now, I stand in awe of the place that God has led me to, knowing that He is faithful to those who trust in Him. I could never have guessed a few years ago that I would be where I am today. It is so much better than what I could have imagined for myself.

I was born in South Africa and my family immigrated to Australia when I was ten. We were a very wealthy and affluent family who had a dark secret. My father was a powerful and brilliant doctor when he was around others, but when he was at home, he was an extremely manipulative, violent, and abusive man who would continually abuse my mother. I adored my mother, and I was very scared of my distant father.

When we moved to Australia as a family, my mother and youngest sister went back to South Africa for eight months to sell our houses and belongings. During that time my grandmother looked after us because my father was so busy living his double life that we never saw him. It was during this time that I would have recurring dreams about him cheating on my mother. Later on, we discovered that my father was an extremely promiscuous man, and my dreams were unfortunately reality.

A few months after my mother arrived back in Australia, my father abandoned us and stole all our money. We were left in a foreign country with nothing but broken hearts. It was in this darkest hour that my mom reached out to God. She introduced a regular Bible study and family prayer time. We spent an hour and a half each morning before school seeking God as a family. We did this for about two-and-a-half years. This was a defining moment in the life of our family. It was during this time that I saw God do miracles in our lives, including feeding us one week when we had only $10 for food. I learned to trust God, and He became my best friend. God was more real to me than anything else in my life, and nothing was ever going to change my mind.

I made friends at high school but I was very reserved and shy. I excelled at athletics and I got very good grades, but I had the reputation of being a "goodie two shoes." I desperately wanted to live for God, and to me that meant being good, but soon this was not enough and I developed an identity crisis. I started imitating the popular people around me, and as a result I was insecure and unsure of myself. This went on for a few years. One day God spoke to me and revealed that He had made me the way He wanted me. He said that I could spend the rest of my life trying to be a lousy someone else, or I could choose to become the best me! From that moment on I got a boldness that I had never before experienced. I came out of my shell and began to discover that I was someone special in my own right.

But after a few years I neglected my relationship with God. I became angry at being ridiculed for being pure, innocent, moral, and doing the right thing. I became angry with God because I thought it was His fault. At eighteen I rebelled against most of what I knew was right and started dating a non-Christian guy, going to parties, getting drunk, and going clubbing to see what I had been missing out on. I was not impressed by what it meant to be "cool" by the world's standards, but I liked the feeling of finally fitting in.

In my final semester at college, I got a scholarship to study in America. This was like a dream come true for me. I spent a year in America studying and working. It was during this time that I let my hair down. I felt like I could earn my independence and finally lose my reputation of being naïve. My housemates were wild and crazy individuals. I joined in and partied hard for a few weeks before I began to notice how broken their lives really were. They all smoked pot every day, and some of their friends were addicted to heroin. One of them was a stripper who had had countless abortions and was constantly being harassed by her abusive boyfriend. The others would sleep with countless men during the same period of time and take drugs such as horse tranquillizers and nitrogen gas just to get high. I was disgusted by what I saw, and I started to drift away. I noticed how selfish they were when I got sick and was in bed for three days, and not once did they ask me how I was. I started spending a lot of time at my other friends' houses to avoid the nauseating scenes I would see at my house. Apart from getting drunk, I never allowed myself to get involved with their lifestyle. I was like a visitor looking in on their lives. It was during this time that I truly discovered what it meant to be me. I discovered what was important to me, what I believed, and what I was never willing to compromise. I saw how the Devil was ruining people's lives all under the disguise of having a good time. It made me sad, and I realized that I had lost my first love. I felt God's gentle call on my heart, and I could resist Him no longer. When I arrived back in Australia, I started serving God with everything I had. I have not stopped since and never will. I have lived life with God and without Him. I have seen both sides of life, and I choose God. There is nothing as satisfying and fulfilling as living for God.

Since I made the decision to live for God, He has opened doors for me that I could only have dreamed of. I got a job as the marketing officer at Curtin School of Design, and I am now the sales and marketing manager for a very successful software company. I know this is just the beginning because God has given me a glimpse of where He is taking me, and it is far greater than what I could have ever planned. He is bringing to pass in my life the passions and desires that have always burned within me. God is bringing to pass a destiny that is far greater than me, a destiny that will bring glory to Him and will further His kingdom on earth. None of this is because of my doing but because I have trusted God. He rewards those who diligently seek Him, and He brings to pass the desires of our hearts.

Let's Pray

Father,
I thank You that You have blessed me with so much. I pray that I will look after the money You give me in a wise and frugal manner. Lord, I pray that You will bless me financially so that I can be a blessing to others.

treasure tip

Indulgent Egyptian-Style Pedicure

Frugality doesn't mean that you have to miss out on the royal treatment. And since your hands have been pampered, it's time to give some attention to your feet. This pedicure will leave you feeling totally luscious but, best of all, it won't cost you a fortune.

Here are five easy steps to leave you walking like an Egyptian:

1. Remove any nail polish on your toenails. Use nail clippers and an emery board to shape toenails into a clean, squareish shape.

2. Soak feet in a large bowl of warm water for a few minutes, then scrub the soles of your feet with a foot file, loofah, or pumice stone. Towel dry your feet.

3. Fill up the bowl again with some warm water, a half-cup of whole milk, a sprinkling of rose petals or other scented flowers, and a few drops of olive oil. Relax and soak feet for 10 minutes. (Milk contains lipids and other properties that soften and deeply condition your skin. No wonder Cleopatra soaked in it. But make sure it's the full-cream variety; skim milk just won't do the trick.)

4. Lightly dry feet and then slather with a rich lotion. Mummify your feet by wrapping them in plastic cling wrap and then put on some thick socks. Pop in a relaxing CD, get a plate of yummy goodies, and just chill out for twenty minutes. Unwrap feet and massage in any excess lotion.

5. Wipe any lotion off your toenails. Pick a color and paint on one coat at a time, waiting until one is dry before doing another or you'll get those nasty little bubbles in the polish. When as many coats as you want are dry, put on a good top coat for gloss and protection.

Voila! Perfect Egyptian footsies!

She sets about her work vigorously; her arms are strong for her tasks.

chapter 7:
barbie and bootylicious bodies

"'It must be inconvenient to be made of flesh,' said the Scarecrow, thoughtfully, 'for you must sleep, and eat and drink. However, you have brains, and it is worth a lot of bother to be able to think properly.'"

THE WIZARD OF OZ (BY L. FRANK BAUM)

Proverbs 31:17

"She sets about her work vigorously; her arms are strong for her tasks."

She is beautiful, smart, and talented!

Her professional ability knows no bounds, and she's worked as a doctor, dentist, scientist, schoolteacher, astronaut, actor, and aviator. She's a billionaire and owns mansions, countless sports cars, helicopters, and speedboats. She's never been married but has been in a committed, long-term relationship with a strong and sensitive guy. She has her own fashion label and is renowned as a style trendsetter.

Her body is described as perfect and has been immortalized on clothing, bed linen, bags, and accessories. She's internationally famous and immensely popular. In fact, she is so celebrated that she is known simply by her first name...Barbie!

In 2001, Barbie's global empire grossed $5 billion. But although she is meant to inspire us with her academic, financial, and personal achievements, it's really her body that we're most interested in, and it's her body that's to die for...literally. You see, if Barbie were a real woman, her bodily dimensions could not sustain her.

She'd have to walk on all fours due to her proportions. Her enormous breasts would literally topple her over, and her ridiculously long, thin legs would physically not be able to support her.

Her swanlike neck would snap from the sheer weight of her hair-heavy head, and little children would scream in terror at her saucer-sized eyes. She would suffer serious breathing problems because her impossibly pinched-in waist indicates that she's had at least a couple of her ribs removed. And of course she wouldn't be able to have children because she'd be too thin to menstruate.

It's impossible for Barbie to be real, and it's impossible for us to ever achieve her bodily dimensions.

Yet that doesn't stop seemingly perfect women from spending thousands of dollars pumping up their chests, de-pumping their thighs, and whittling down their waists. The truth is, we are a society obsessed with the body and making it bodacious, beautiful, and (in the words of Destiny's Child) bootylicious.

However, God doesn't want us to be obsessed with our bodies. Instead we need to have a healthy attitude toward life and how we look after our bodies. When I read in Proverbs about our 31 girl, I find that she possesses a healthy attitude toward her body. In Proverbs 31:17, I picture a girl who is robust, healthy, full of vigor, energy, and vitality. It says that she goes about her work energetically, and her arms are strong for her tasks. She's definitely no fragile flower; in fact, she is in good physical shape!

It's important that we look after ourselves and treat with care the body God's given us. God wants our bodies to be healthy and strong but not to be propped up on a pedestal to idolize.

First Corinthians 6:19–20 says, *"Do you not know that your body is a temple of the Holy Spirit, who is in you, whom you have received from God? You are not your own; you were bought at a price. Therefore honor God with your body."*

This Scripture is specifically referring to sexual sin and not defiling our bodies with sexual immorality. However, the truth is that we can abuse and defile our bodies in ways other than sexual sin.

By deliberately starving ourselves, overeating, binging and purging, not exercising, and not getting enough sleep, we are ruining, vandalizing, and destroying our bodies...God's temple.

So how do we look after our bodies and honor God with them? How do we get them in good physical shape like the 31 girl? Let's take a look at some areas:

You Are What You Eat
Food is such an important part of our lives; it's the fuel that keeps us alive and healthy. Yet many girls use and abuse their bodies with food or the lack of it.

In our western world, eating disorders are at epidemic proportions with anorexia, bulimia, and compulsive overeating. But when food stops being an ally to our health and becomes a tool to control ourselves, an addiction, or a source of comfort and security, then we're abusing the very thing that God intended for our good.

In her book *Reviving Ophelia,* author Mary Pipher descriptively details the effects of eating disorders on girls. She details how anorexia slows down the metabolism, causing a person to be lethargic, irritable, and tired. The skin, hair, and nails become dull and lifeless. It can trigger serious fainting episodes and cause periods to be irregular and eventually cease, which in turn can cause infertility.[4] Anorexia may enable girls to lose weight, but the price they pay is incredibly high.

Pipher goes on to describe how bulimia is also a serious health issue. The constant vomiting causes stomach acids to rot and discolor the teeth; the acid also causes throat and gastric problems. Most serious of all, though, bulimia can cause electrolytic imbalances that can trigger heart attacks.

Anorexia and bulimia are serious health issues. There is definitely nothing attractive about any of these disorders, and by sowing them in our lives, we will reap health problems.

By being obsessed over the need to have a better body and being eager to please others by attempting to look picture-perfect, we basically lose our unique identity. To put it simply, we have sold our souls in an attempt to have the ideal body, certainly something God never intended for His beautiful girls.

Overeating is also a serious problem. Girls who use food as a drug that takes away boredom, pain, loneliness, confusion, or anxiety are on a dangerous road, which will lead to problems with obesity.

It is far better to learn how to deal with these emotions with the help of God and friends instead of using food as the solution to life's problems.

Pipher also shares the wisdom of the Overeaters Anonymous acronym **HALT**—Don't get too **H**ungry, **A**ngry, **L**onely, or **T**ired. She states the importance of identifying your feelings and not labeling everything as hunger. She advises you to learn to rest when you're tired, not to bottle up anger, tell someone how you feel, and to find something (other than eating) to do when you're lonely or bored.[5]

Food should be our ally, not the enemy. The key to healthy eating is moderation, and including foods from all five food groups.

Imagine the change in our lives if we loved ourselves as we are! So take a look at yourself—be happy with who you are and what you have to offer the world—and go out and do it! (WOMENSPORT WEST)

real life
Laura's Story

I was brought up in a Christian home, but when I entered my senior year in high school, things started to spiral out of control.

I had always been a good student and reasonably popular, but my self-esteem was at an all-time low. I thought that if I changed the way I looked, I would be happy. So I started to diet and increased the amount of exercise I did every day. I was a girl yearning to be loved—yearning to fit in and willing to do anything to achieve it. Little did I know that I was walking further and further away from God, the only One who could love me unconditionally. Eventually, things began to slip. What was a diet, now became an obsession. I was determined to cut out all fat from my diet, and I was skipping meals constantly. If I thought that I had eaten something that was going to cause me to put on weight, I would attempt to throw it up. I remember sometimes sitting in my bathroom, crying because I couldn't vomit up something I had eaten half an hour earlier.

I started to get sick. My metabolism dropped to an all-time low, because I was skipping lunch every day. I didn't get my period for twelve weeks straight. I became anemic (low iron count), and things were not much better socially. I went from one boyfriend to another, searching for love and never finding it. I compromised on my boundaries, and although I never had sex with any of them, I compromised my purity.

On the outside, I looked like a girl who had it all. Boyfriends, popularity, and good grades. I became real good at hiding the truth, but on the inside I was slowly dying.

It was at the end of eleventh grade when God intervened in my life. My cousin told me about a youth camp she was going to. I was interested and asked if I could come. As it turned out, I got the last spot available. Talk about a God moment! And on the first night of camp, I returned home to my heavenly Father. I asked Jesus to enter my life and be the center of my world. I felt complete. I was loved unconditionally, no matter what I looked like.

Things in my life changed from that point on. Of course, it didn't happen overnight, as life is a journey. But the great thing was that I wasn't walking it alone anymore. I was walking hand in hand with my Father. It hasn't always been easy, but even in my darkest days, He is there comforting and protecting me. I have been blessed so richly by Him. He has surrounded me with people in my life who are constantly strengthening me. He has taught me to find my happiness and security in Him. What can I say? I am a girl in love with my Lord and Savior!

(Girls, please remember that eating disorders are deadly serious, and if any of you are having problems in this area then talk to someone you trust—a leader, friend, parent, or doctor. Get some help because you don't have to go through it by yourself.)

Get Physical

It's important to keep fit. Exercise not only increases your metabolism and assists in your body functioning well, but it can also help to clear your mind, flush out toxins, increase your bone density (which delays the onset of osteoporosis), and give you loads more energy. But the key is to keep a healthy attitude toward exercise and not get obsessed with it.

The goal should be fitness, not necessarily looking better. If your goal is to look better, then the reality is that you will never be truly satisfied. There will always be something about yourself that needs to look better—thinner thighs, a smaller bum, or tighter abs.

When I was in my teens, I became obsessed with exercising. What started out as a couple of aerobic sessions a week turned into a crazy need to be reed thin. I ended up going to the gym seven days a week and doing a minimum of two aerobic classes a day. My goal was to look good, but I was never satisfied with the results.

I was convinced I still needed to tone up (even though I could easily put my hands around my waist), and many times I would leave the gym depressed and frustrated at myself because I still didn't look good enough. Thank goodness I got over it and got myself a life! Now I exercise primarily to increase my fitness and level of well-being.

To maintain a good level of fitness, it is recommended that you exercise three to four times a week for a minimum of thirty minutes each time. So do something you enjoy! There's no point doing something that you hate because you won't maintain it. Start an exercise program today that you can maintain and that you love doing. Better still, exercise with a friend. You'll have fun and work out your jaw muscles too!

Rest 'n' Recreation

Your body needs sleep, and it's important that you get at least eight hours of sleep a day. While you're sleeping, your mind and body can rejuvenate so you're able to function well the next day. Lack of sleep can cause loss of concentration, irritability, skin problems, general lethargy, and tiredness.

However, too much sleep (i.e. ten to twelve hours) can also cause you to be tired and lethargic. So the key is around eight hours sleep a night.

Recreation is also important to maintaining a healthy body. In fact, you've probably heard of the term **recreational activity**. But it's very easy to get so busy that you forget to "recreate" yourself, and that's simply what *recreational* means—re-creating yourself.

So what leisure activity is it that really makes you feel great, alive, and refreshed? For me, it's simply going to the markets and browsing around. I hardly ever buy anything, but what I really love to do is see, touch, and smell the market goodies. I always come away feeling energized. It's crucial to unwind and recharge your batteries. Whatever "recreates" you, make sure that you do it at least once a week.

Remember, what you sow, you reap. You may not reap it tomorrow or even in a month's time, but you will eventually reap. The unhealthy lifestyle you sow today will reap you an unhealthy life in the years in to come. Make a decision today to live a healthy life and honor God with your body.

There is definitely nothing attractive or God-honoring about being weak, sickly, unhealthy, or lethargic, especially if you can do something about it. So take a page out of Proverbs and get in good physical shape!

Let's pray

Father,
I thank You for the body You have given me. Please forgive me if I have misused and abused it. My body is a temple of Your Holy Spirit, and my desire is to honor You with it.

treasure tip
Have a Healthy Self-Image

We should all aim to work toward being content in our own skin. Here are some tips toward having a healthy body image: [6]

1. **Waiting until you have the perfect body to feel good will not bring you happiness.** Confidence, being well groomed, good posture, and being positive, energetic, and interested in others are features most often reported in people considered attractive—not body weight.

2. **Don't get focused on the dial on the scales.** Health, fitness, self-care, and a balanced diet are better measures of health and weight management than weight alone. Instead of setting weight goals, set fitness or health-related goals.

3. **Buy and wear clothes for the way you look now.** You are more likely to look after your body if you feel you look good than if you wait until you feel good about your body.

4. **Look after and nurture your body.** Don't focus on punishment and deprivation. Have a bath, take a walk, paint your toenails, care for your skin, change your haircut, or pursue a new hobby. Self-care, not self-punishment, is the fastest way to weight management and feeling better about your body.

5. **Don't define yourself by your weight.** Ask yourself how you want loved ones to remember you and aim to improve these personal characteristics. Body shape is usually one of the last attributes by which you will be remembered.

6. **Live for today because life is "how you live each day."** Don't think that tomorrow will be different if you are not prepared to look after your body today.

7. **Ask yourself how much of your time is spent thinking about your body image.** What is acceptable to you, and is this representative of your priorities in life?

8. **Be gentle with yourself and be positive in your self-talk.** Remember the days when you felt good about yourself, how motivating it was? Being negative about your body makes it less likely, not more likely, that you will achieve your goals.

out at night. In her hand she holds the distaff and grasps the spindle with her fingers. She sees that her trading is profitable, and her lamp does not go out at night. In her hand she holds the distaff and grasps the spindle with her fingers. She sees that her trading is profitable, and her lamp does not go out at night. In her hand she holds the distaff and grasps the spindle with her fingers. She sees that her trading is profitable, and her lamp does not go out at night. In her hand she holds the distaff and grasps the spindle with her fingers. She sees that her trading is profitable, and her lamp does not go out at night. In her hand she holds the distaff and grasps the spindle with her fingers. She sees that her trading is profitable, and her lamp does not go out at night. In her hand she holds the distaff and grasps the spindle with her fingers. She sees that her trading is profitable, and her lamp does not go out at night. In her hand she holds the distaff and grasps the spindle with her fingers. She sees that her trading is profitable, and her lamp does not go out at night. In her hand she holds the distaff and grasps the spindle with her fingers. She sees that her trading is profitable, and her lamp does not go out at night. In her hand she holds the distaff and grasps the spindle with her fingers. She sees that her trading is profitable, and her lamp does not go out at night. In her hand she holds the distaff and grasps the spindle with her fingers. She sees that her trading is profitable, and her lamp does not go out at night. In her hand she holds the distaff and grasps the spindle with her fingers. She sees that her trading is profitable, and her lamp does not go out at night. In her hand she holds the distaff and grasps the spindle with her fingers. She sees that her trading is profitable, and her lamp does not go out at night. In her hand she holds the distaff and grasps the spindle with her fingers. She sees that her trading is profitable, and her lamp does not go out at night. In her hand she holds the

a girl

chapter 8:
what you see is what you get

"*Griselda opened her eyes. What did she see? The loveliest, loveliest garden that ever or never a little girl's eyes saw. As for describing it, I cannot. I must leave a good deal to your fancy. It was just a delicious garden.*"

THE CUCKOO CLOCK (BY MRS. MOLESWORTH)

Proverbs 31:18–19

"She sees that her trading is profitable, and her lamp does not go out at night. In her hand she holds the distaff and grasps the spindle with her fingers."

Have you ever been so excited about something that you just couldn't sleep?

It could have been the night before a performance, vacation, Christmas, or a trip overseas. Your mind was racing, you felt tingly, butterflies were doing somersaults in your stomach, and maybe you even felt a little nervous. And no matter how hard you tried, your mind just wouldn't slow down; counting sheep was useless because they were running around in your head at one hundred miles an hour!

As frustrating as this can sometimes be, it's also invigorating to be so excited about something that you cannot sleep. To have a vision that keeps you wide-awake, alive, and fresh.

In Proverbs 31:18–19, we find our 31 girl is working late into the night because she *"sees"* what she does is profitable, productive, and valuable. Her hands are literally busied with her vision. She's excited, passionate, and spurred on. And my question to you, 31 girl, is "What's your vision? What keeps you awake at night? What are you prepared to work hard at because you can see that it's profitable and, furthermore, beneficial?"

Is it a vision to run your own business, or be a journalist, teacher, designer, or engineer? Maybe you want to travel or work as a volunteer abroad helping others. Wherever your path in life takes you, it's important that you have a vision to take you there. A vision that keeps you alive and, in return, fuels you with desire and hope.

Charles Swindoll said, *"Vision is essential for survival. It is spawned by faith, sustained by hope, sparked by imagination, and strengthened by enthusiasm. It is greater than sight, deeper than a dream, broader than an idea. Vision encompasses vast vistas outside the realm of the predictable, the safe, the expected. No wonder we perish without it!"*

The Bible makes it very clear that we need a vision in life. Proverbs 29:18 says, *"Where there is no vision, the people perish"* (KJV). A vision sustains us and keeps us grounded. In fact, if we have a vision we will put on restraints or disciplines in our life to fulfill that vision.

For example, if you have a vision be a doctor one day, then you will need to put boundaries and disciplines in place to ensure that you get the grades through high school and college. You definitely can't watch television all night or go out partying all week. There are sacrifices that you will need to make, but if you believe strongly enough in it, then the sacrifices won't be burdensome.

Here are some things you need to understand about vision:

Make God the Foundation for Your Vision
It's important that your vision lines up with the unique plan that God has designed for your life and that you see it as part of His "big picture." When you open your eyes and see that your life can impact many other lives around you, then that's when your vision really becomes exciting. In other words, when you stop living simply for your own little desires and live for God's cause, that's when your vision takes on purpose. And there's nothing better and more invigorating than living for something bigger than yourself.

I heard once that vision is looking at life through God's eyes. When you have the courage to do this, your vision literally explodes into something bigger, brighter, and more brilliant than you could ever imagine.

Connect Your Vision to the Local Church
I remember a girl in our youth ministry who was incredibly talented, smart, and outgoing. In fact, anything she touched turned to gold. She was gifted in sport, music, and study. Whenever I would talk to her, she would tell me how her vision was to be a missionary and evangelist one day. She said she loved God. However, she put all her talent into areas other than the church. Although she was a great musician, she never once played in the church or joined the youth worship team. Her sports team, school music team, and debating team took priority over coming

to youth group on Fridays or cell group twice a month. In fact, there was always something more important to attend, and church was definitely not a priority. God had been gracious to bestow her with talent, beauty, and brains, yet sadly she never gave her gifts back to further His kingdom and never sought to connect her vision to the church.

The truth is the local church needs a girl like you! It needs your passion, talent, time, and treasure. Many times we have a vision but we never seek opportunities on how to connect it with the church. The Bible says in Matthew 6:33, *"But seek first his kingdom and his righteousness, and all these things will be given to you as well."* When you make God and His church a priority in your life, then He blesses you with much more than you ever desired. So look for opportunities to serve. All it takes is a heart that's obedient to God and committed to His church.

Keep Your Vision Alive
Don't let your vision shrivel up and die. Keep it alive! Nourish it, protect it, and fuel it. Nothing will kill your vision more than making wrong choices. The choices you make will either move you closer or further away from your vision. Sometimes those choices will be difficult, painful, and even frustrating, but in the end you'll fulfill what you were always born to do.

It's also hard to keep your vision alive if your friends or the people you hang out with don't support your vision. Get around people who share your passion and have a similar vision. Only tell people your vision if you know they're not going to ridicule or knock you down because of it. It's hard enough to believe in yourself without your friends not supporting you too.

Finally, keep the vision alive through your imagination. Your mind is a powerful tool, and you can keep your vision alive by throwing the fuel of imagination upon it. Every so often, get yourself in a quiet place and just let your imagination go wild. Dream about that day when you graduate college with a degree in marketing or medicine. Or when you start working in your chosen field, whether it's teaching, hairdressing, computing, or science.

We grow **great** by **dreams**....Some of us let these great dreams die, but others **nourish** and protect them; nurse them through bad days till they bring them to the **sunshine and light** which comes always to those who sincerely **hope** that their dreams **come true.** (WOODROW WILSON)

real life
Jen's Story

Ever thought you were pretty average? I did!

Who would have thought that my life would pan out the way it has? Some would say it's just a fluke, but I disagree. It's the hand of God directing my path.

When I was three, my mom enrolled me in our local dancing school, Beverley Margaret School of Dance. I was just your average little dancer who didn't have a real talent for it and was definitely never going to be a prima ballerina! But I really loved my dancing and always had heaps of fun doing it.

School didn't interest me very much, and I wasn't super academic. Again, I was pretty average at it. And sports was never my thing (actually I really hated it), so I didn't really know what I was going to do when I grew up.

Tap was my favorite type of dance, followed by classical, then jazz. As I got older, I became more and more dedicated to my dancing. By the time I was fourteen, I was student teaching and pretty much lived at the studio. My mom suggested that I shift my bed down there.

Around this time a series of events occurred that turned my world upside down. My grandma, Nanna, died in November 1994. Then the following May, my parents separated, and a few months after that, my cousin committed suicide. There were times when I felt like giving up on life because it all seemed too hard. But luckily I had support from my family and people and teachers at the dance school, which helped me through.

All my life I've been a Catholic, but I was never really involved in church or interested— in fact, I found it quite boring. But I remember being about sixteen and sitting at the back of church with this dream of one day opening my own dancing school; I wanted to name it Footprints. I never really paid much attention to it; besides, it was a dream. I wasn't good enough to open my own school.

Life rolled on and I graduated from high school. I was working full time and teaching whenever I had a spare moment. Dancing was my life. I loved it. Not long after this I started attending Riverview Church. I cut back on my dancing a little bit to get more involved and to attend Bible college. It was at church that I realized this dream that I had could possibly be part of my destiny. Those seeds and thoughts were planted in me by God.

I started to question whether I could really open my own Christian-based dancing school. I struggled with this question for a long time. There was always an excuse, and one day I just decided it was never going to happen and gave up on the whole idea. Besides, it was me just dreaming.

But I still pondered all the time about opening my own school. Then about six months later I decided (after praying and speaking to friends and family) to give it a go. I decided I had nothing to lose and everything to gain. All I knew was that I didn't want to wake up when I was forty thinking, "What if I had?"

So I did it! February 23, 2002, Footprintz Dance Academy opened. On my first day I had about twelve students, and it was brilliant. I'm very blessed. I have my own studio at the back of my aunty's dance shop and the full support of my dancing teacher (who I still teach for). The school is growing every week, and I have BIG goals and dreams for it. I want to impact and change the face of dancing schools in Perth, outreach through my dancing school, and touch those people who have not yet met their Maker.

Don't despise the day of small beginnings. All I can say is "you ain't seen nothing yet!"

Seek to serve God first and watch how He brings the dreams in your heart to pass. Dream big, dream often, and dream wildly!

Let's pray

prayer

Father,
My desire is to seek Your ingdom first and for You to be the number one priority in my life. I pray that You expand me so that I see life through Your eyes. Lord, I lay all my dreams and desires at Your feet and commit my ways to You.

treasure tip
Period Pain

It can sometimes be hard to dream and envision your future when you're living in the reality of everyday life. And although I love being a girl, I have to say that one of the most bothersome realities about being a girl is getting my monthly period. Periods are inconvenient, annoying, and uncomfortable!

But if you find that period pain is stopping you from living life well, then you can do something about it.

Here are a couple of tips:

- **Exercise**—When you've got your period, exercise can be the last thing you want to do. But doing light, low-impact exercise like stretching, walking, or swimming can actually help ease cramps. I've also found doing sit-ups (yes, I know it's hard to believe) can also help.

- **Primrose Oil**—Primrose oil is a great help. It's the seed oil extracted from the evening primrose flower. Health professionals praise its benefits and say it can help reduce premenstrual symptoms such as cramping and mood swings. You can purchase primrose oil capsules or tablets from a health food store or pharmacy.

If period pain is more than just slight discomfort and if you find yourself in agony, then you may have a menstrual disorder. Please see your doctor if you suffer from severe menstrual symptoms that leave you in pain and disrupt your lifestyle.

Remember, periods don't have to stop you from leading a normal, healthy life. In fact, if you've seen some of the ads on TV, then you know that feminine hygiene products can actually empower YOU to save the world and all its inhabitants...yeah, I wish!

She opens her arms to the poor and extends her hands to the needy. She opens her arms to the poor and extends her hands to the needy. She opens her arms to the poor and extends her hands to the needy. She opens her arms to the poor and extends her hands to the needy. She opens her arms to the poor and extends her hands to the needy. She opens her arms to the poor and extends her hands to the needy. She opens her arms to the poor and extends her hands to the needy. She opens her arms to the poor and extends her hands to the needy. She opens her arms to the poor and extends her hands to the needy. She opens her arms to the poor and extends her hands to the needy. She opens her arms to the poor and extends her hands to the needy. She opens her arms to the poor and extends her hands to the needy. She opens her arms to the poor and extends her hands to the needy. She opens her arms to the poor and extends her hands to the needy. She opens her arms to the poor and extends her hands to the needy. She opens her arms to the poor and extends her hands to the needy. She opens her arms to the poor and extends her hands to the needy. She opens her arms to the poor and extends her hands to the needy. She opens her arms to the poor and extends her hands to the needy. She opens her arms to the poor and extends her hands to the needy. She opens her arms to the poor and extends her hands to the needy. She opens her arms to the poor and extends her hands to the needy. She opens her arms to the poor and extends her hands to the needy. She opens her arms to the poor and extends her hands to the needy. She opens her arms to the poor and extends her hands to the needy. She opens her arms to the poor and extends her hands to the needy. She opens her arms to the poor and extends her hands to the needy.

31 July

chapter 9:
the easiest thing to do is nothing

"A little Consideration, a little Thought for Others, makes All the Difference."

THE COMPLETE TALES OF WINNIE THE POOH (BY A. A. MILNE)

Proverbs 31:20

"She opens her arms to the poor and extends her hands to the needy."

Once upon a time, a king had a great highway built for the members of his kingdom. After it was completed, but before it was opened to the public, the king decided to have a contest. He invited as many as desired to participate. Their challenge was to see who could travel the highway the best.

Many people competed and traveled along the highway all day, but each one, when they arrived at the end, complained to the king that there was a large pile of rocks and debris left on the road at one spot, and this got in their way and hindered their travel.

At the end of the day, a lone traveler crossed the finish line wearily and walked over to the king. He was tired and dirty, but he addressed the king with great respect and handed him a bag of gold. He explained, "I stopped along the way to clear a pile of rocks and debris that was blocking the road. This bag of gold was under it all. I want you to return it to its rightful owner."

The king replied, "You are the rightful owner."

The traveler replied, "Oh no, this is not mine. I've never known such money."

"Oh yes," said the king, "you've earned this gold, for you won my contest. *He who travels the road best is he who makes the road smoother for those who will follow."*

This story was written by an unknown author and is a great example of generosity. When we think of generosity we usually equate it with giving money, but generosity is far more than just giving financially. A truly generous person literally gives of herself. And that's what the traveler in the story did. He was more interested in making the road easier, smoother, and safer for other travelers than finishing first or fastest. He gave up the desire to win and instead gave of his time and energy to ensure a safe journey for others.

Proverbs 31:20 paints a picture of the 31 girl as generous and giving. The Bible tells us that she gives to the poor and needy. She opens and extends herself to those who are desperate. And friend, God wants His girls also to be generous. John 3:16 says, *"For God so loved the world that he gave his one and only Son."* Our God is a generous, giving God. He gave His absolute best to us, and He wants us to give our absolute best to Him and to others.

To be generous, however, takes effort. In fact, it's far easier, safer, and less costly to do nothing and be indifferent. But by doing nothing we miss out not only on God's blessings but also on reaping a rewarding, exciting, and fulfilling life. It's when you give that you truly begin to live.

So how do you develop generosity in your life?

Learn to Be Content
We live in a very materialistic culture and almost every advertisement you watch on television is trying to sell you something. Our world is not satisfied with what it's got. It wants and must have more clothes, jewelry, cosmetics, shoes, or accessories. It's very easy to get sucked into the lie that to be worth something you've got to be drinking the latest drink or wearing the coolest label. Our culture demands that we never be satisfied with what we've got. And it's this greedy appetite for "stuff" that is totally opposite to the quality of generosity.

Contentment comes from the heart, but if you are filling your heart with the desire for possessions, then you have a problem. Contentment and greed cannot exist together, so you need to stop feeding your appetite for possessions. Here are some tips to help you:

a. Don't get sucked into the lie sold by fashion magazines. Fashion magazines have only one goal, and that is for you to buy and be seen in the latest fashion. Reading these magazines only gets you conned into thinking that you "must have" the latest look for the latest season. Now there's nothing wrong with wanting to be fashionable, but don't swallow the **"must have"** bait, or you'll be hooked.

b. Don't go to the mall or shopping center when you're bored or have nothing to do. Going shopping will only make you want and long for more, and chances are you'll end up buying something that you don't really need.

c. Add some depth to your life and expand your conversational repertoire by reading about stuff other than fashion, music, and entertainment. Realize how shallow it is to be consumed by material things and how fortunate you are to simply have a home and food to eat. It's important to put things into perspective and know that there are bigger issues at stake. Ultimately you need to realize that the world will keep spinning even if you haven't got the new season's "must have" skirt.

Develop the Habit to Give

Generosity is a habit you learn. Richard Foster said, *"Just the very act of letting go of money, or some other treasure, does something within us. It destroys the demon greed."* Generously volunteering to give yourself in an area within the church or community will help toward cultivating a generous spirit. So don't be stingy and tight-fisted with your treasure, talent, or time.

Be Compassionate

Proverbs 31:20 says that *"she opens her arms to the poor and extends her hands to the needy."* Notice it doesn't say that she keeps her arms folded and closes her hands! Obviously this girl is moved by compassion. It compels her to be generous to those around her. And that's what compassion should also do for you. True compassion never causes you to remain indifferent or stand still. Compassion should compel you into acting generously. It's this compassion that compels you to give to charity organizations, and it's compassion that should compel you to give to God's cause.

When we have a genuine love for people it will move us to open our arms and extend our hands to those without hope, without answers, and without a Savior.

I want to leave you with a quote by John Bunyan: *"You have not lived today until you have done something for someone who can never repay you."*

Our heavenly Father generously gave us the gift of eternal life, which we can never repay. As God's daughter, I hope that you also choose to be like Him and live a life that generously gives to others who can never repay you.

Let's give unselfishly, with pure motives, and with clean hearts just like the 31 girl.

Let's Pray

Father,
I thank You from the depth of my heart that You loved me so much You gave Jesus as a sacrifice for my sins. I thank You that now I will spend eternity with You. I pray that each day You will give me the opportunity to give to others who can never repay me and that each day I will grow to be more like You.

treasure tip

The Best Things in Life Are Free!

Being content with material possessions is all about realizing that the best things in life really are free. Just looking at life with a contented, grateful heart makes you see things differently.

Here are some BEST THINGS sent to me over the Internet by my friend Katrin:

- Laughing so hard your face hurts.
- A hot shower in winter.
- Getting encouraging mail.
- Taking a drive along the coast.
- Lying in bed listening to the rain outside.
- Hot towels fresh out of the dryer.
- Hot bread straight from the oven.
- Finding the sweater you want is on sale for half price.
- Chocolate milkshake (or vanilla, or strawberry, or banana, etc.).
- A bubble bath.
- A good conversation.
- The beach.
- Finding $20 in your coat from last winter.
- Running through sprinklers.
- A pillow fight
- Best friends.
- Blowing bubbles at a child.
- Accidentally overhearing someone say something nice about you.
- Waking up and realizing you still have a few hours left to sleep.
- Seeing all the newborn ducklings in spring.

Now it's your turn. Why don't you see how many things you can come up with. Enjoy the best things in life and be content!

When it snows, she has no fear for her household; for all of them are clothed in scarlet. When it snows, she has no fear for her household; for all of them are clothed in scarlet. When it snows, she has no fear for her household; for all of them are clothed in scarlet. When it snows, she has no fear for her household; for all of them are clothed in scarlet. When it snows, she has no fear for her household; for all of them are clothed in scarlet. When it snows, she has no fear for her household; for all of them are clothed in scarlet. When it snows, she has no fear for her household; for all of them are clothed in scarlet. When it snows, she has no fear for her household; for all of them are clothed in scarlet. When it snows, she has no fear for her household; for all of them are clothed in scarlet. When it snows, she has no fear for her household; for all of them are clothed in scarlet. When it snows, she has no fear for her household; for all of them are clothed in scarlet. When it snows, she has no fear for her household; for all of them are clothed in scarlet.

31:21

chapter 10:
an ant's life

"There was a Camel, and he lived in the middle of Howling Desert because he did not want to work; and besides, he was a Howler himself. So he ate sticks and thorns and tamarisks and milkweed and prickles, most 'scruciating idle; and when anybody spoke to him he said, 'Humph!' Just 'Humph!' and no more."

HOW THE CAMEL GOT HIS HUMP (BY RUDYARD KIPLING)

Proverbs 31:21

"When it snows, she has no fear for her household; for all of them are clothed in scarlet."

Dogs are smart little cookies.

My grandfather once had a German shepherd who used to bury the house keys for him. He didn't want to carry his keys in case he lost them so when he got home, all he would do is give the dog the command, and she would dig them up for him. Pretty clever!

But there are lots of other animals apart from dogs that are also clever. Monkeys, elephants, dolphins, and even pigs are actually smarter than dogs. They are the Einsteins of the animal kingdom. However, God doesn't mention these so-called smarty-pants in the Bible. Instead He asks us to ponder the humble little ant.

So what's so special about this insignificant insect that many of us would rather stomp on than notice? Well, apart from the fact that they had a movie dedicated to them (*Antz*), they also have something in common with our 31 girl. You see, ants prepare themselves for the hard times ahead. They gather their food in summer and at harvest so that there's plenty of food in winter. They're not fearful of winter when there's no food around because they've been busy during summer. Far from being lazy, they've stored up for themselves a smorgasbord of yummy goodies that will ensure they don't go hungry during the cold spell. And that's exactly the mind-set of the 31 girl.

It says in Proverbs 31:21 that she's not afraid when it snows because she's prepared. Everyone in her household is warm and clothed in scarlet. Now I'm not suggesting that you go out and purchase some red trench coats for you and your family before winter sets in. I am suggesting however, that you prepare yourself for the hard times ahead so when they come, there's no need for you to be afraid.

James 1:2–4 says, *"Consider it pure joy, my brothers, whenever you face trials of many kinds, because you know that the testing of your faith develops perseverance. Perseverance must finish its work so that you may be mature and complete, not lacking anything."*

Those of you who want to be mature, complete, and not lacking anything—hands up! I certainly do! Imagine that, NOT LACKING ANYTHING!

The bare bones facts are that you will face hard times, challenges, trials, and tests. The question to ask is, "Will you end up stronger or weaker because of them?" I'm hoping you'll end up stronger. The key to remember, though, is you need to prepare yourself. It's no good pretending "it'll never happen to me" or hiding your head in the sand. The 31 girl is not afraid of the cold times ahead because she's prepared. And the same should be said of us.

So how should we prepare ourselves in life?

Prepare Yourself Spiritually

During tough times it's your faith that gets tested. And the only way your faith is going to weather the storms of life is by being strong. The Bible says that faith is increased by hearing the Word of God.

The Word of God adds bulk and muscle to your faith. That's why it's so important to read God's Word and spend time in His presence. I've said it before, but I'll say it a million times again—you've got to spend daily time with God by yourself!

Read and digest His Word, pray to Him, and worship Him. By doing this daily you will not only build up your faith muscle but also build a firm foundation upon which you can stand when life socks you one.

real life
Melody's Story

I've grown up in a Christian family so I've known God all my life, but it wasn't until five years ago that I really experienced His comfort and found Him to be my greatest friend.

In September 1996 my beautiful mom passed away after being in a coma for a year. This was such a dark and difficult time in my life. I felt lonely and alone.

I didn't understand why this had happened to my family, and the big question was why God didn't heal my mother. It was a painful, confusing, and distressing time.

During this time I had to fully trust and rely on God to get me through to the other side, which He did. I am so thankful to Him for giving me and my family the strength to carry on and live day by day. Through all this I've learned that the best friend you can ever have to trust, love, depend upon, and who will always be there by your side even when you are going through hard times is Jesus.

I have also learned to honor my dad, who, through all these years, has trusted God and never once doubted Him. He has been a true inspiration to my brothers and sisters and me. I know if it hadn't been for my dad's strong faith in God, we wouldn't have made it through.

Jesus is truly the best friend I've ever had and will have, and through the death of my mom I have learned that each trial we go through prepares us for the rest of our lives.

Prepare Yourself Emotionally

Everyone has weaknesses in life. Weaknesses such as temper outbursts, jealousy, insecurity, lust, and indulging in gossip. If you don't deal with these weaknesses, they will cause you to become stuck in life. You can deal with weaknesses by first recognizing and admitting that you have them. Second, it's important to hand them over to God and ask for His help in dealing with them. Third, tell someone about them so they can hold you accountable.

If you're emotionally prepared and strong, you will be better equipped to handle life's hurdles when they come your way.

Prepare Yourself Physically

Your body is not invincible. It won't last if you don't treat it well. Too many times people reach their thirties and forties and suffer from the habit of a poor diet and lack of exercise that they formed in their teens and twenties.

And when we get sick, it takes us longer to recover because we're not healthy in the first place. Treat your body well so that it's better prepared when you face times of stress or sickness.

Prepare Yourself Financially

In the chapter "Money, money, money," I shared the importance of being money-wise and of developing the habit to save for your future. Too many times we live thinking only about today. We waste our money on things that don't even last. It's much wiser to cultivate a habit of putting something aside each payday or when you get pocket money. If saving becomes an ingrained habit in your life, then when you're older you'll never be unprepared when unexpected bills, challenges, or opportunities come your way.

Preparation in life is important. When the storms of life come our way, we're not going to end up being shipwrecked casualties. We've built our foundations, and we've prepared ourselves spiritually, emotionally, physically, and financially. Just like the 31 girl who has no fear of the cold times because she's prepared herself, you too will be prepared.

You are God's royal daughter, destined for greatness and well prepared for life's challenges.

Let's Pray

Father,
My desire is to be mature, complete, and not lacking anything. I know that when hard times come, You will be with me and help me through to the other side. I can do all things through You because You strengthen me.

treasure tip

Laughter Is the Best Medicine

When you're going through the "winters" of your life, it's easy to get stressed and overwhelmed. You know the feeling: Your heart is racing, your head hurts, you get irritable, and you can't sleep well. But stress can be alleviated simply by laughing. Yes, that's right, laughter really is the best and cheapest medicine.

When we laugh, we release endorphins in our body that give us a natural and totally safe "high." In fact, the medical profession tells us that we should be laughing at least eight times a day. This habit will actually prolong our lives and can help keep us healthy. Pretty cool!

So here are ten suggestions to ensure you get a good chuckle every day:

- Rent a funny video.
- Read a joke book or surf online for a joke website (make sure it's clean).
- Laugh at yourself by seeing the funny side of your mistakes.
- Make silly faces at yourself in the mirror.
- Talk to young children.
- Get a friend to tickle you mercilessly.
- Spend time with people who make you laugh.
- Start an Embarrassment Journal where you write down your most embarrassing moments in life and read them regularly.
- Take part in a karaoke night (especially if you can't sing).

Life is too short to waste on being worried or stressed. Get healthy and happy by overdosing on regular laughter sessions, and most importantly don't take yourself so seriously!

How we spend our **days** is—of course—how we spend our **lives**. (ANNIE DILLARD)

She makes coverings for her bed; she is clothed in fine linen and purple.

Beauty

31

chapter 11:
the princess's new clothes

"He was always changing his clothes, sometimes a dozen times a day and, although most rulers are to be found in their council chambers, this Emperor was always sure to be found in his wardrobe!"

THE EMPEROR'S NEW CLOTHES (BY HANS CHRISTIAN ANDERSEN)

Proverbs 31:22

"She makes coverings for her bed; she is clothed in fine linen and purple."

I love fairy tales, and *The Emperor's New Clothes* is one of my favorites.

It's the story of a vain emperor who loved the latest fashion. As the story goes, he was duped by con men who promised to dress him in the latest threads. They claimed they would make the emperor an outfit from the most beautiful material imaginable. However, this material could only be seen by people who were intelligent. The scam was that this material did not even exist. But not wanting to seem stupid, everyone pretended to see the clothes when in fact there was nothing.

The story ends with the emperor parading down the streets "nikky-noo-naa" (that's naked) in his supposedly "new" clothes. It took a young child, with all the innocence and honesty that only a young child has, to point out that the emperor was, in fact, stark naked! Eventually others also pointed out that the emperor wasn't wearing any clothes. The emperor finally realized he'd been tricked. He wasn't wearing clothes at all, but he continued his parade down the town catwalk to everyone's amusement. Brave guy!

The emperor was prepared to go naked just so he didn't appear stupid and unfashionable.

Fast-forward to the 21st Century. The fashion world dictates what we should wear if we want to be "WITH IT." Just like the emperor in the fairy tale, it's easy for people to also get duped into wearing the latest fashion, even if it's unflattering, absurd, or inappropriate. And nowadays we are told that it's not enough to be attractive, but we must have sex appeal too.

Fashion these days screams sex. We have teeny-weeny tops with messages such as *Flirt, Sexy, Sex Goddess, Tart,* and *Vixen* emblazoned on them. Clothing stores have racks of how-low-can-you-go hipsters, skirts that look more like belts, and pastel-hued hot pants. "Must have" accessories are belly-button rings to go with that buffed belly.

But clothing stores aren't the only ones promoting the "dress sexy" message; it's also interesting to note the headlines in popular women's magazines. "101 Ways to Dress Sexy," "Must-Have Sexy Looks for Winter," "How to Be Sexy," "What's Sexy Now," "The 20 Sexiest People in the World," and "Sexy at Any Size."

I can only come to one conclusion: Our society is obsessed with the need to be sexy, and we are bombarded with the message that to be attractive, we have to dress sexy, act sexy, and exude sexy!

However, in Proverbs 31:22 we discover the story of a princess and her new clothes. I love this Scripture because it shows me that God knows us girls well. He knew that if He was going to describe a girl that He wanted us to aspire toward, then He'd better put in something about fashion!

In Proverbs 31:22 we find that the 31 girl is one stylish babe! It tells us that not only is her bedroom dressed in style but so too is she. *"She is clothed in fine linen and purple."* In ancient times, purple and fine linen were symbols of royalty. She knows she's a princess, and she dresses like one. Forget sex appeal. She has royal style appeal!

So here are a couple of points to remember next time you're deciding what to pick for your royal attire:

Don't Be Swindled

Over a hundred years ago, the 1888 winter publication of the fashion guide *Ladies Guide to Health* advised young men to wear warm woolen pants, jackets, and sweaters. Young women, on the other hand, were advised to wear floaty silk and feminine lace, so as to expose their lovely arms and shoulders. Consequently many girls (more concerned with looking good than shivering in the snow) died from pneumonia. Although this fashion advice seems ridiculous, I've lost count of the number of times I've been out to dinner in freezing conditions only to see shivering, scantily clad girls. I don't know what they were thinking, but a mouth full of chattering teeth, a red runny nose, and blue frozen skin is not a good look under any circumstance!

And from the crippling foot-binding practices of China to the insane gridiron-looking shoulder pads of the '80s, women throughout the ages have had dictated to them what to wear and how to look.

The fashion intelligentsia have demanded that we sacrifice ourselves on the altar of fashion and forgo being comfortable, relaxed, and even warm in winter!

But it's time to revolt against such nonsense and use some common fashion sense:

a. Don't swallow the lie that to be attractive you need to be showing off your body in tight, revealing clothing. You will probably get noticed, but it may not be the type of attention you want. Your smile, personality, and mind are what make you appealing, not your clothes. (And if it's cold outside, wear something warm!)
b. Don't get pressured by fashion magazines into wearing what's "in" now. Instead employ the services of a brutally honest friend and ask her whether the latest season's "must have" items are flattering or faltering. It's highly unlikely that every new fashion fad will suit you. So be selective and style savvy.

Are You Stylish or Sexy?
It is possible to dress fashionably without dressing sexy. Now I don't want this to be about what you should and shouldn't wear, but it is important for us girls not to be naïve toward the "sexual pull" we have when we dress in certain ways.

Next time you get dressed to go out, ask yourself the question, "Do I feel stylish or sexy?" If you're unsure, then delve a little deeper. To be stylish means *fashionable, chic, tasteful, classy, trendy, smart,* and *elegant.*

To be sexy means *seductive, provocative, sensual,* and *erotic.* Breaking it down into these two groups of words makes it easier to define.

If you deliberately dress in a sexy way, you need to ask yourself why. "Why do I need to look and feel sexy? Why do I need to be the object of desire? Why do I need the attention of guys?"

Usually you will find that if you need to feel seductive and sexy, then there are some deeper issues that perhaps need to be dealt with. I certainly don't want to trivialize these issues, but the bottom line is that you don't NEED to be the object of a guy's desires or fantasy because you already are the object of God's desire. You have His undivided attention, love, and adoration. Put simply, you are irresistible to Him.

Psalm 45:11 says, *"The king is enthralled by your beauty; honor him, for he is your lord."* Imagine that: Your beauty is enthralling to God! A guy may not always find you attractive, but be secure in the fact God is forever rapt with you!

It goes on to say in verses 13 and 14, *"All glorious is the princess within her chamber; her gown is interwoven with gold. In embroidred garments she is led to the king."* Do you get the picture? You were born for greatness. As God's daughter you are royalty. That means you are priceless and invaluable. Don't cheapen your value by your dress code. Dress with your worth in mind.

We started off this message by talking about the *Emperor's New Clothes.* The simple fact (or fairy tale) is that the emperor was conned into wearing nothing out of his need to be attractive. My desire is that you don't follow in his footsteps by wearing next to nothing because you want to be attractive too.

In the words of Sandra Bullock in the film *28 Days, "Don't be anyone's slogan, for you are poetry."*

Alyson's Story

There comes a time in the life of every honest young girl when she feels totally alone. This feeling usually doesn't last long—a couple of days, weeks, even months, are bearable. In my teenage experience, loneliness was a horrible ongoing battle that lasted throughout most of my high school life—a monster that would rear its ugly head, regardless of how many friends I had or how many parties I was invited to. I often felt totally isolated, even though, to the casual observer, I would probably have looked like I had no problem being accepted. Popularity is one thing, but the ongoing struggle to accept yourself is another thing altogether.

To say I was a late bloomer when it came to discovering the mystery of the opposite sex would be a huge understatement. I had my first real 'crush" at sixteen and didn't get a boyfriend until I was nearly seventeen. In my circle of friends, this made me seem like someone with a major disease and I grew very uncomfortable being the terminal "nun." While it was true that the romantic interest of the male species was a totally foreign phenomenon in my life, I still craved the acceptance and self-worth that came with knowing a boy was interested in me.

Then one day in eleventh grade, it happened. A guy I was really good friends with in my chemistry class began to take enormous interest in my life. At the same time, an older guy I knew, who was quite popular and good-looking, began to notice my existence—sending me flowers, buying me gifts, inviting me to parties, and introducing me to his friends. This was a completely new but very welcome experience for my totally naïve and flawed self-esteem.

All this sudden attention did incredible things for my sense of self. I became addicted to the feelings that come with male attention. I found myself desperate for a boyfriend, but when I got one, I quickly got bored and began to search for a new "interest" in my life. It was like a craving that would never go away.

Although I was not a serial dater, I had a number of casual male acquaintances who I knew were interested in pursuing a relationship with me. So I would make them my bait, using their friendship when it suited me, and only until the next real "catch" came along. By the time I was in my late teens I had only had one long-term relationship (it lasted six months), but I consistently craved new "love interests," regardless of whether I had any intention of pursuing them or not. This caused my boyfriend immense pain, though he rarely indicated his frustrations. We remain firm friends to this day, but often when we reminisce about that time, I feel incredible remorse for the way I treated him!

Then when I was nineteen, my world came crashing down around me. My two best friends in the universe went on tour for a year with a youth evangelization team. Although I was happy for them, the feelings of loneliness and isolation I had often battled with began to consume me. I had known one of these friends since I was seven years old, and with their departure came a sense that my whole stability and security had been rocked. In my very immature and insecure view, they were not leaving Perth, they were leaving me.

At the same time I found myself in a relationship that was emotionally and mentally harrowing and caused me to feel even less worthwhile at times. I was struggling at college, not so much in my grades but in my desire to attend. I would skip classes regularly and had lost my passion for learning and achieving new things. My relationship with my parents, which had so often been such a wonderful respite for me in earlier years, had become increasingly difficult as my boyfriend became my entire world.

Toward the middle of that year, I moved in temporarily with my sister, and it was during this time that I finally began to realize the damage I was doing to myself and the people I loved. I was growing more and more distant from my true friends, and I also realized I had to end my current relationship. I had always taken great comfort in *my relationship with God and His forgiveness and unconditional love. Now, I felt as though I had become spiritually dry—that God was so far away no matter how much I tried to reach Him. Ironically I couldn't seem to shake this unwavering desire to enter into full-time youth ministry. I began to attend Bible college in the hope that somehow God could redeem my flawed self and make the dream a reality.*

Something else happened that year that, in hindsight, changed my destiny forever, and even at that embryonic stage in my spiritual development, would have an incredible impact on my life. I met the quiet, awkward, incredibly shy young man who would eventually become my husband. Neither of us could have had any indication of the eight intense, sometimes harrowing, often unpredictable years it would take for me to become "wife material." It was a journey of rediscovery, instability, and at times, great sacrifice on both our parts. Two-and-a-half years into our relationship, I realized I could no longer go on the way I was. Marcus and I ended our relationship, and I began the next part of the journey that would see me spend three years learning to be whole without a guy by my side. To say that Marcus was blessed with incredible patience as he waited for this insecure, immature little girl to emerge into the woman of God she dreamed of becoming would be an incredible understatement!

More and more as I searched myself and asked God to shed light on my flaws and insecurities, I began to realize the incredible seductiveness of this thing we call "innocent flirtation." Flirting has many faces—the innocent batting of the eyelashes, the provocative dress that shows just enough skin, the playful brush past our intended "target," that seductive, lip-glossed pout, or that sideways gaze that lingers just long enough to send a signal. But flirting is much more than this too. It can become an addictive behavior that is both deliberate and voluntary. It is an attempt to assert power over another individual for your own benefit, to make you feel popular, wanted, or adored, regardless of the mixed messages and wrong perceptions that your actions may send to the other person.

My adult life has been a pilgrimage of healing. A journey of learning to accept myself wholly and completely before I could ever give myself to another human being. A lesson about the kind of woman that changes her world, and about learning to become that woman in a way that honors self, respects others and glorifies God.

Life has become an incredibly satisfying adventure. I am living my dreams—married to an amazing, godly man who treats me as a precious and rare treasure. Together, we eagerly await the birth of our first baby and share our life with friends and family who continually remind us of the simple joys of life. I enjoy the privilege of ministering to a youth generation who restore my faith in this world every day. And I pursue God with all my heart, eager to share His message of grace, hope, and unconditional love.

It's a beautiful way to live.

Let's Pray

prayer

Father,
I pray that I will recognize You as my source of security, love, and comfort. My desire is to be a pure princess in my thoughts, actions, and the way I dress.

Pimple Problem

Your best "look" is not your trusty Levi 501s or designer T-shirt; it's your skin. Yes, that's right, healthy skin is your best accessory in life. But when you're going through adolescence and hormonal changes, it's your skin that can become your worst nightmare.

Here are some tips that may help you cope:

Tip 1

Clean your face morning and night with a cleanser or non-soap product. Avoid cleaning your face with hot water because it will only make your pimples worse. Instead, shower with warm water or, even better, clean your face at a sink. The key is not to steam your face as this will result in overstimulating your skin and only make the redness worse. If your pimples do not improve, try using a medicating face wash from your local pharmacy. You may need to try a few different face washes before you find the one that suits your skin type.

Tip 2

Makeup clogs your pores and makes them more prone to pimples, so avoid wearing too much makeup. If possible wear makeup only on special occasions. If you need to wear makeup regularly, then use a foundation that is light or just apply a concealer. And no matter how tired you are, always remove your makeup before you go to bed.

Tip 3

Research has shown that the foods you eat will not give you pimples. But a healthy diet can definitely improve the condition of your complexion.

Tip 4

Don't squeeze! Squeezing pimples can result in scarring and it can also cause infection by forcing debris and oils deeper into the skin. Rather than improving your complexion, it actually makes it worse.

The problem with pimples is that they really are primarily based on your hormones. Even if you've got a great skincare routine, you eat healthy, and you're not a stress-case, you can still get the dreaded pimple. Your best bet is to use products that help you heal quickly.

and

31

at among the elders of the land. Her husband is respected
e city gate, where he takes his seat among the elders of the
nd. Her husband is respected at the city gate, where he tak
s seat among the elders of the land. Her husband is respect
the city gate, where he takes his seat among the elders of t
nd. Her husband is respected at the city gate, where he tak
s seat among the elders of the land. Her husband is respect
the city gate, where he takes his seat among the elders of t
nd. Her husband is respected at the city gate, where he tak
s seat among the elders of the land. Her husband is respect
the city gate, where he takes his seat among the elders of t
nd. Her husband is respected at the city gate, where he tak
s seat among the elders of the land. Her husband is respect
the city gate, where he takes his seat among the elders of t
nd. Her husband is respected at the city gate, where he tak
s seat among the elders of the land. Her husband is respect
the city gate, where he takes his seat among the elders of t
nd. Her husband is respected at the city gate, where he tak
s seat among the elders of the land. Her husband is respect
the city gate, where he takes his seat among the elders of t
nd. Her husband is respected at the city gate, where he tak
s seat among the elders of the land. Her husband is respect
the city gate, where he takes his seat among the elders of t
nd. Her husband is respected at the city gate, where he tak

chapter 12:
big on the inside

"'Simba, remember who you are,' said the voice of Mufasa. 'You are my son, and the one true King. You must take your place in the Circle of Life.'"

THE LION KING (BY DISNEY)

Proverbs 31:23

"Her husband is respected at the city gate, where he takes his seat among the elders of the land."

In the previous chapters, you've been reading about the awesome 31 girl. You've learned about her faithfulness, diligence, self-discipline, and many other qualities. Now it's time to find out a little bit about the man she's married to.

The Bible says that her husband is a respected member of society. In fact, he's a leader and key influencer in the city. He's important, honored, and trustworthy. Although this Scripture is not directly about the 31 girl, it does reveal a lot about her character.

You would agree with me that the girl you've been reading about is talented, smart, and godly. Yet she's not the one who is a mover and shaker in her city. It's her husband that takes on that prestige.

Now some people may protest, "How unfair! She's the one who's brilliant, financially sharp, and hardworking. Shouldn't she be the one who's elevated to a position of authority and leadership?" Perhaps. But this Scripture beautifully reveals a girl who is incredibly secure in God and mature in her outlook. Not only that, but she's obviously someone who brings out the best in those around her, namely, her husband.

You see it takes a big-hearted person to be genuinely happy when friends succeed and are given opportunities to excel. It takes a girl who is incredibly secure in herself and God to overcome resentment, envy, and jealousy and to help others grow and reach their potential. It would be quite understandable for the 31 girl to complain and whine about why she isn't given the opportunity to lead like her husband, but instead she's a girl with a gorgeous attitude who actually enjoys helping others excel. Yes it's hard to believe, isn't it!

And rather than complain and grumble about why we weren't given the opportunity to represent our school in sports, sing in the band, or star in the school play, God wants us to model this girl and also have a secure attitude toward seeing others succeed.

In fact, He wants us to be proactive in our friendships and bring out the best in people around us. Now, this may be a big ask (especially when someone else gets something that we've always had our heart set upon), but the Christian walk is never going to be an easy one.

So here are a couple of challenges that we all need to face:

Don't Compare Yourself to Others
When we compare, we despair. Let's face it, someone else is always going to be more beautiful, more talented, and smarter than us. The sooner we accept this unchangeable fact and celebrate our uniqueness, the sooner we are able to genuinely see others as a blessing rather than a threat.

One of the most reassuring and beautiful Scriptures in the Bible is Psalm 139:13–14, which says, *"For you created my inmost being; you knit me together in my mother's womb. I praise you because I am fearfully and wonderfully made; your works are wonderful, I know that full well."*

You need to realize that God, with His awesome power, has incredibly crafted and fashioned you.

You are perfect, unique, irreplaceable, inimitable, matchless, exclusive, exceptional, distinctive, and absolutely priceless to Him! Accept it, believe it, and be secure in His love.

Danica's Story

I was brought up in a pretty normal family. I am the oldest of three, and although none of my family is Christian (YET), they all hold typical Christian ideals and norms—just minus the God factor. My upbringing was very family-orientated with no major traumas.

By the time I reached the final years of elementary school, my friends meant a lot to me. I began to seek my self-worth based on their attitudes toward me. I loved to be around them and went out with them almost every day.

Eighth grade was a huge change for me. No longer was my little friendship group exclusive. My friends began to find other friends from different schools. They started to become judgmental and mean. Slowly the acceptance that I craved from them started to dry up. They became nasty to everyone who refused to go along with their games, including me. They began to abuse me both physically and verbally. I would just sit there wearing a brave face and take it as my self-esteem plummeted. I watched my supposed "best friend" turn her back on me. After many weeks of teary walks home, I gathered up the courage to leave them. I was left feeling betrayed, empty, unworthy, and lonely.

One day an old friend of mine who had also suffered from the torment of these girls told me about a book she had been reading. The book was on New Age movements and witchcraft. This intrigued both of us, and we became more and more involved, giving the Devil a larger and larger part of our hearts. We went to a gathering, checked out the witchy shops, and basically immersed ourselves in it as much as we could. I won't go into it now because the thought of it all still makes me feel so sick and sorry to God. Looking back now it is so obvious to me that I was doing this to fill the hole in my heart and to win the acceptance of my friend. All this time my search for "distant" powers seemed so far away. Instead of a relationship with the ONE God, I sought different gods in order to fill the different needs in my life. I was convinced that if I had the right herbs and right hour of the day I could get a god's attention somewhere to somehow meet the need I felt I had. I felt I was trying and trying but still falling short.

Thankfully I never did anything too drastic. However, through all of this I was developing a strong self-dependency, relying and trusting in only myself. At about the same time my aunt invited me and my cousins to a youth rally being held in our neighborhood. I showed up so unaware of what I was in for! The whole time I was there it became so obvious to me that these people had something I didn't have. There was an awesome atmosphere of acceptance, unity, and joy. What were these people so happy about? What did they have to celebrate? Inside, I spotted a girl from school. I didn't really know her, but she said hi to me and disappeared. Most of the rally was a blur of people, loud music, and a longing to relate. Then a guy got up in the front and talked about how our actions affected others. This message really hit home. As he did the altar call, my heart was beating at a million miles an hour. I rushed forward along with hundreds of others. I can still remember scanning the crowd and seeing a couple of girls from school with huge smiles, clapping and cheering for me. That night I gave my life to Christ and was forgiven of all my sins. I was given a clean slate and a fresh perspective on life. I became aware that God knew my past but, more importantly, had plans for my future. I was given a reason to live other than for myself. I still thank God today that He rescued me right when I needed saving. His timing is so divinely full of purpose.

That was almost four years ago, and it hasn't been all smooth sailing. I turned my back on those friends I had tried so hard to impress. I surrendered the control I felt I had to have in my life over to God's care. It took me about two years of twice-a-week chaplain visits to find the real me and slowly begin to trust people not to hurt me. I'm still not completely there yet, but I know God's got it all under control. He has rebuilt my confidence and self-esteem. God hasn't protected me from obstacles but has given me a way through them. God has also put some wonderful friends in my life who accept me for me and are teaching me so much; I am so blessed to know them. And as for those girls I felt I had to try to impress, I have forgiven them and am now slowly rebuilding our friendships and openly talking to them about God! Who ever said the unimaginable cannot happen? We go through everything for a reason. Life is all about lessons, and you never know how God is going to use the test you are going through now to bring glory to Him.

I am now a leader in our youth ministry's junior high program and have a passion for young girls as I know firsthand how going into high school can damage self-esteem. I desperately want to teach and nurture these girls to become beautiful, strong, passionate women after God's own heart.

Psalm 144:12 has lately become the song of my heart, and it goes a little something like this: "May our daughters (that's you and me) be like pillars (strong, built on solid foundations) carved down (soft to God's Word) to adorn (add beauty to) a palace." You might think of pillars as huge fat hunks of plaster, but think about it; without pillars the palace would fall down. I also believe that the palaces that God means here are not only ones where royalty live but could also represent families, workplaces, and relationships.

God sees us as so important He wants us to not only be strong women who hold together the palaces of the world but to also add beauty to them! So be encouraged that no matter how you see yourself, God sees potential in you. He has a job for us to do, and so often we need remind ourselves to stand tall and pillar-like for Him! You never know what palace God wants to build around you.

Encourage Unconditionally

It's simple for us to encourage and support others when they are talented in areas that we're not. The challenge comes when God asks us to encourage and be supportive of people who have the same gifts as us. For example it's easy to say, "That's great!" to your friend who was successful in joining a local band when you don't have a musical bone in your body. But how tough is it to smile and be happy when you've been putting in extra time and money for drama classes and it's your friend who gets chosen to play the lead in a play and you have to settle for the part of an extra. Desire to be the type of girl who encourages regardless, and allow God to transform, soften, and grow your heart.

Believe me, bringing out the best in others can be one of life's greatest thrills. So pour out your encouragement and support onto those around you, and enjoy the adventure ahead!

Let's Pray

Father,
I thank You that You created me unique and priceless, and I rest in You, knowing that You love me unconditionally. Grow my heart and help me be a source of encouragement, love, and support to others.

treasure tip
Bath Time Bliss

If we live our lives encouraging, helping, and spoiling other people, then there is no need to feel guilty when we spoil ourselves too. And if there's one way to thoroughly spoil yourself, it is in a heavenly bath. So get ready for some guilt-free indulgence:

1. Switch off as much external noise as possible by turning off the TV and taking the phone off the hook (and gagging your little brother).
2. Make sure the bathroom is at a nice temperature. It's no fun going from a warm bath back out into a freezing environment.
3. Create soft, relaxing light by burning some candles or smaller tea lights and placing them around the bathroom.
4. Get moody and play some music that will create the relaxed vibe you want.
5. Drink a cup of herbal tea. Chamomile is the most dreamy choice. But if you want to feel refreshed and energized, then peppermint or citrus is a good alternative.
6. Ensure the water is just right. If you have a cold and want to detox, then very hot water is good (no more than 98 degrees F). If you have sensitive or dry skin, then go for a lukewarm bath but, if you're game for an energy boost, then try a cold one.
7. As the water is filling up, put in some of your favorite bath salts or a bath bomb. But for something really beneficial, why not swirl through some essential aromatherapy oils? (Check out the Treasure Tip at the end of Chapter 15 for the lowdown on aromatherapy oils.)
8. Just chill out. You should try to soak in the bath for at least five minutes but no more than twenty minutes (unless you want to look like a shriveled prune).
9. Once you've finished your bath, gently pat dry your skin. If you've put essential oils in your bath they will continue to be absorbed into your skin. Next generously slather skin cream all over to ensure your skin is well moisturized.
10. Now for the best bit. Put on some comfy sweatpants, soft fluffy socks, and settle down with a good book, CD, or video, and you'll be amazed at how fresh and relaxed you feel!

A long hot shower may be great, but a soak in the tub is absolutely scrumptious!

She makes linen garments and sells them, and supplies the merchants with sashes. She makes linen garments and sells them, and supplies the merchants with sashes. She makes linen garments and sells them, and supplies the merchants with sashes. She makes linen garments and sells them, and supplies the merchants with sashes. She makes linen garments and sells them, and supplies the merchants with sashes. She makes linen garments and sells them, and supplies the merchants with sashes. She makes linen garments and sells them, and supplies the merchants with sashes. She makes linen garments and sells them, and supplies the merchants with sashes. She makes linen garments and sells them, and supplies the merchants with sashes. She makes linen garments and sells them, and supplies the merchants with sashes. She makes linen garments and sells them, and supplies the merchants with sashes. She makes linen garments and sells them, and supplies the merchants with sashes. She makes linen garments and sells them, and supplies the merchants with sashes. She makes linen garments and sells them, and supplies the merchants with sashes. She makes linen garments and sells them, and supplies the merchants with sashes. She makes linen garments and sells them, and supplies the merchants with sashes. She makes linen garments and sells them, and supplies the merchants with sashes.

chapter 13:
get arty

"There is something about midnight meals that makes people have clever ideas. Sure enough, on the stroke of twelve, Marilyn Hawthorn suddenly thought of the answer to her problem."

THE RUNAWAY REPTILES (BY MARGARET MAHY)

Proverbs 31:24

"She makes linen garments and sells them, and supplies the merchants with sashes."

There are some parts of the Bible I seriously struggle with.

Scriptures that talk about loving people who hurt and use us, finding joy in the trials of our lives, forgiving and forgetting other people's mistakes, and funnily enough Proverbs 31:24.

You see, I was never much of a seamstress, and the idea of making sashes, scarves, or shirts just never happened for me. Oh, I tried to do it. I enrolled in a Janome sewing course, hoping to graduate as a designer of haute couture. But after presenting my family with crooked-collared shirts and misshapen pants, I faced the fact (to my family's delight) that it was never going to happen. In fact, I confess that I can't even sew on a button! Obviously that course was a complete waste of money.

However, I've come to realize that Proverbs 31:24 is not necessarily about dressmaking but more about creativity. You see, our God is unbelievably creative, and it's a quality that He desires to see in His girls too.

Now some of you may be thinking, "That's just not going to happen for me. I'm just not the arty type." Well, allow me to let you in on a little secret...if you are a human being, you were born to be creative. The Bible says that we were created in the image of God. Our God is creative and, as a result, we inherited the creativity gene. It's in our DNA!

So what exactly is creativity? To me, it's being *"divinely inspired to make our world a better place."* Many times people get intimidated by this creativity thing. They think because they can't paint, draw, sculpt, make lovely pottery, or arrange flowers that they're not creative.

However, don't believe the lie that you are not creative, for you have been created by God, the author of Creativity. Proverbs 31:24 simply shows us the creativity of a girl who uses her talents to enhance her world.

Ted Engstrom stated, *"Creativity has been built into every one of us; it's part of the design. Each of us lives less of the life God intended for us when we choose not to live out of the creative powers we possess."* [7]

I absolutely love it when my young son has done a painting or made something for me at his playgroup. I proudly show off his creative efforts to my friends and display his artwork on my fridge or in my office at work. And I like to think that it's the same with God.

Whenever you use your creativity to make your world better, He absolutely loves it. In fact, I bet there's an art gallery in heaven where He lovingly displays your creative efforts for all the angels to ooh and aah over.

The challenge we all face is to actively develop that creativity and tap into those ideas that are waiting to be unearthed. Creativity takes effort, and some of the world's best inventions and ideas came from someone taking the time out to improve their world.

One of the biggest creativity-killers is television because it is a totally passive activity. It doesn't encourage thinking or response, and it actually dulls our creative senses. In fact, sleeping is the only thing you can do that is less active than watching TV—and even then, you dream.

So how about turning it off! Since 1995, one week every year has been set aside as **National TV Turnoff Week** in America. Can you imagine that—a week without TV! Some of you are probably suffering heart palpitations just thinking about missing out on your favorite shows!

But instead of freaking out and going cold turkey, you can start by having certain days of the week as TV-free days.

Now with the box off, you can fill your mind and time with whatever gets your creative senses stimulated. Why not read a great book, write a poem, paint, or draw. Remember what it's like to simply imagine, dream, pretend, and make believe.

Go outside, lie on the ground, and find shapes in the clouds (I bet you haven't done that in a while). Without the distraction of TV, you are able to discover what feeds your creativity. It could be going for a walk in the park, listening to music, or browsing the markets and knicknack stores. Perhaps it's even in doing the mundane (weird but true), like chores or riding the train. In fact, some of my best ideas have come from washing the dishes and driving in my car!

Turning off the TV really could end up being the best creative decision you've made in a while.

Brooks Atkinson said, *"Everyone can achieve a great deal...according to the burning intensity of their will and the keenness of the imagination."* [8]

So how determined are you to be successful and make your world better? Just imagine, in each of us there are creative ideas just waiting to improve our world. So take the time to unearth them, dust them off, polish them up, and present them.

Imagination and **creativity** are more **important** than knowledge.
(ALBERT EINSTEIN)

Amanda's Story

From a very early age, I knew that I would give my life to the service of God. I was brought up in a Catholic home, and so my only understanding of serving God in a full-time capacity was by becoming a nun. This confused me for such a long time because I couldn't understand how God had placed this deep desire in my heart to work for Him, yet the only way I thought I could was by giving up so much! (To a young mind, no sex, husband, children, or family was soooooooooooooo much! Plus the whole dress sense thing!)

Therefore I put these thoughts of serving God full time down to a childish fantasy and fervently launched myself into a career of becoming the next big musical theater star! I trained six days a week in dancing, drama, and singing. I ate, slept, and breathed musicals. I spent eighteen years of my life trying to fill the void in my heart with the high that audience applause inevitably gives all of those who live for the theater.

When I was fifteen, I started my own business. I taught dance, drama, and singing in high schools, elementary schools, and my creative arts school. I got into college before I finished high school through an interview and audition process. I did a degree at the Western Australian Academy of Performing Arts in Musical Theater. I also did a BA in English/Comparative Literature and History. I had a contract with Warner Brothers and performed in their shows. I sang on television, performed in professional musical theater shows, and directed a youth theater show on AIDS that won awards.

All of this sounded so exciting, and I loved shocking people with all that I had done in such a short space of time. However, I now realize that circumstances of my life made me grow up very quickly, and my achievements were totally about people thinking I was a good person rather than achieving to learn more or to gain knowledge. My study was never about myself, it was about what others thought of me. This need to overachieve stemmed from the fact that I was abused when I was younger, and this experience infiltrated and totally warped my self-perception and drastically affected my self-image.

This created a spiral in my life. I studied and overachieved so that my family, friends, and even strangers would be proud of who I was and then might begin to think that I was a worthwhile person. However, living this type of life was so demanding because I tried so hard to please everyone. This led to self-destructive habits such as alcohol abuse, drugs, smoking, and eventually an eating disorder that no one knew was totally ruining my life, my voice, and my future! I had become a machine that was working in survival mode, and I hated every part of my being and could never accept that I would be worthy of anyone or anything.

For such a long time I saw myself totally unworthy of love and was so busy doing so much stuff that I had no idea God would love me even if I sat on a beach and did nothing for the rest of my life!

I went out with guys only if I knew that they might like me, because I was so scared of rejection! These relationships were just another way that I could prove how worthy I was of love, yet I never accepted the love or the encouragement that they gave me!

Throughout all of this time I was a Christian, but one who had no understanding of who God actually was. I thought that God was a mean, angry, disciplinarian who no one could please no matter how good they were. So I spent my life doing stuff to please Him too. But no matter how much stuff I did, I was never completely satisfied because I did not have a relationship with God. Everyone around me was so sure that I had everything under control and lived an amazingly fulfilling life. However none of them knew the pain and how broken the real Amanda was. No one saw the person who cried herself to sleep and desperately wanted someone to see how unhappy she was inside. I was a great actress who portrayed a perfect life yet had such a broken one inside.

I eventually came to a place where I was so broken that only God could fix the hurt inside. This process happened the year that I was in Bible College and totally gave my whole life to God, completely! I knew I couldn't act any longer and really needed a Savior to complete my world.

I now live my life totally for an audience of One! I am not perfect, and God is still working on stuff, but I do not care what others think of me and only care whether I am pleasing God! I know that God is watching me in this huge grandstand, and His applause is the best ovation that anyone could ever aspire or hope for. God has healed me and is in a process of daily changing what was broken into a person of strength.

Be divinely inspired and allow God to turn you and your ideas into masterpieces.

Let's Pray

prayer

Father,
Your Word says that I have been made in Your image, which means You have made me to be creative. Lord I desire you to breathe Your creative breath deep within me. Inspire me to make my world a better place.

treasure tip
Mind Games

Next time you get together with your friends, don't turn on the TV, pop in a video, or just read some mags. Why don't you stimulate your mind, do something a little different, and get out some board games.

I know some of you are already thinking, "That is so dorky," but stay with me on this because, believe me, it really can be a lot of fun.

Here are some to get you started:

- Monopoly (guaranteed to reveal the cheats in all of us)
- Scrabble (guaranteed to reveal the smarty-pants in all of us)
- Pictionary (guaranteed to reveal the hidden artists in all of us)
- Balderdash (guaranteed to reveal the fibbers in all of us)
- Yahtzee (never played this one, but I liked the sound of it)
- Chutes & Ladders (okay, maybe forget this one)

If you haven't got any board games, then just go for the old-time classic, Charades. It's guaranteed to have you and your friends giggling uncontrollably.

Anyway these are just some suggestions. But if you're going to have a games night, you've also got to remember the food. And if you're going to get into a food fight, then just remember this tip: the more pudding the better!

So have fun with your friends and remember to play by the rules.

She is clothed with strength and dignity; she can laugh at the days to come. She is clothed with strength and dignity; she can laugh at the days to come. She is clothed with strength and dignity; she can laugh at the days to come. She is clothed with strength and dignity; she can laugh at the days to come. She is clothed with strength and dignity; she can laugh at the days to come. She is clothed with strength and dignity; she can laugh at the days to come. She is clothed with strength and dignity; she can laugh at the days to come. She is clothed with strength and dignity; she can laugh at the days to come. She is clothed with strength and dignity; she can laugh at the days to come. She is clothed with strength and dignity; she can laugh at the days to come. She is clothed with strength and dignity; she can laugh at the days to come. She is clothed with strength and dignity; she can laugh at the days to come. She is clothed with strength and dignity; she can laugh at the days to come. She is clothed with strength and dignity; she can laugh at the days to come. She is clothed with strength and dignity; she can laugh at the days to come. She is clothed with strength and dignity; she can laugh at the days to come. She is clothed with strength and dignity; she can laugh at the days to come. She is clothed with strength and dignity; she can laugh at the days to come. She is clothed with strength and dignity; she can laugh at the days to come. She is clothed with strength and dignity; she can laugh at the days to come. She is clothed with strength and dignity; she can laugh at the days to come. She is clothed with strength and dignity; she can laugh at the days to come. She is clothed with strength and dignity; she can laugh at the days to come. She is clothed with

31 days

chapter 14:
walking tall

"Ride a Cock-Horse to Banbury Cross
To see a fine lady upon a white horse;
Rings on her fingers and bells on her toes,
And she shall have music wherever
she goes."

THE CLASSIC MOTHER GOOSE (EDITED BY ARMAND EISEN)

Proverbs 31:25

"She is clothed with strength and dignity;
she can laugh at the days to come."

Ever since I can remember, I was always the tallest in my class.

I still vividly recall in seventh grade being taller than all of my teachers. One day, a classmate made the smart comment, "If she's this tall now, imagine how tall she'll be when she's twenty years old!" I cried all the way home, absolutely terrified that I'd end up in a circus freak show billed as "The Attack of the Fifty-Foot Woman." But my most embarrassing moment occurred in fifth grade when it came time for the annual class photos.

I always wanted to be one of the petite girls who got to sit on the front row, prettily holding up the class grade sign. But alas, that was never going to be my destiny. Instead, I was always relegated to the back row with the Neanderthals who burped and farted through the entire photo session.

Yet, in spite of my ordeal, I still looked forward to getting the photo and taking it home to my parents. However, this one time I was definitely going to be the class joke. As I eagerly opened up the photo and searched for my picture (as we all do), I was absolutely horrified. There I was, standing on the back row, but because I was taller than everyone else, the photographer (who obviously wanted an even, aesthetically pleasing photo) had cut the top half of my head from the photo.

So there I was, a "half-head," while everyone else had nice full heads, even the Neanderthals! It was then and there that I came to the conclusion that I hated being tall.

That episode occurred over twenty years ago, and you'll be glad to know that I've actually come to terms with my height. In fact, I like being tall. But it's strange how people's opinions and the world's viewpoint can literally "stunt" us. For years I walked around hunched over because I was so incredibly self-conscious of my appearance.

It wasn't until I was in my teenage years, enjoying a relationship with God, that I literally found my confidence, strength, and dignity in Him.

Psalm 3:3 says, *"But you are a shield around me, O LORD; you bestow glory on me and lift up my head."*

This is definitely one of my all-time favorite Scriptures because whenever I read it, I picture a loving and tender Father who gently lifts the heads of His children and desires for them to walk tall and confident. God is saddened when His children are hunched over by the cares of the world and people's opinions. God is the restorer of our souls, and He desires to restore to us whatever has been stolen from us.

When you discover who you are in Christ, you can walk with your head held high and your shoulders back. You can walk with strength and dignity and know without any doubts that God is your heavenly Father, He is the restorer of your soul, and you are His treasured daughter.

Certainly that is the picture that I see of the 31 girl. The Bible says that strength and dignity make up her clothing, and she has a positive outlook on the days ahead. She knows she belongs to God. She is unqualified royalty.

Let's take a look at her signature style in more detail:

Strength
One of the meanings of the word *strength* is potency. This girl is clothed with a compelling, persuasive, and intoxicating faith. When God is real to us and we understand His amazing love, grace, and forgiveness, then we will be compelled to share that with others. It's a heartfelt faith that is contagious and makes us stand out from the crowd. The 31 girl has a relationship with God that literally strengthens, sustains her, and sets her apart.

Dignity
When we are clothed in dignity, we are clothed in regal apparel. Dignity conveys a sense of stateliness, majesty, and true worth.

The 31 girl knows she is valuable and priceless to God, and as such, she lives her life with her head held high in confidence. It's not a conceited confidence centered on the "Girl Power" manifesto or the media's message of "Girls Rule!" but rather a grateful assurance in knowing that she has been adopted by God; her Father is the King of Kings, and she is royalty. Dignity comes when we have a transforming encounter with our heavenly Father, the indisputable liberator, empowerer, and encourager of all time. He is the lifter of our heads!

Positive Outlook
The 31 girl laughs at the days to come. Basically, this means that she looks forward in anticipation to the days ahead. She's not worried about getting older, whether her family will be safe and secure, or about the challenges ahead. She can laugh at the days to come because God is her sense of security, stability, refuge, and reliance.

The Bible clearly tells us not to worry about the future because God, who considers us infinitely more valuable than the birds and the flowers, will look after us. Worry has no benefits in our life but rather causes stress and health problems. The Bible says that God has inscribed us on the palms of His hands, and He will never forget or forsake us. (See Hebrews 13:5.) In essence, God will always be there for us.

I hope that you have been encouraged in knowing that you too can be clothed in strength and dignity. You can have a relationship with God that is contagious and intoxicating to others around you. And rather than worry about your future you can look forward to it in anticipation and excitement, knowing that your heavenly Father has you securely and safely in the shelter of His hands.

Written by one of the masterpieces in our youth ministry is the following poem, which aptly describes each and every single one of us.

Masterpiece

Your light shines like a candle in the dark
To lead me my way and show me my path.
You're all I need to brighten my day
In each and every single way.
You planned me carefully, each little hair.
Created a partner to be my pair.
You gave me feelings for them to share,
To cry, to love and a sense to care.

You crafted my face each little dimple,
A face one day that will be filled with wrinkles.
You gave me mistakes for me to learn from,
A friend on those days for me to lean on.

You gave me your Word, a book to read,
And helped me in all my times of need.
You showed me a way out of the dark
And lit up my life like a lamp on a path.

(SABINA BERNSMAN)

Let's Pray

Father,
I thank You that You are the restorer of my soul. You restore to me strength and dignity, worth, and honor. I cast all my worries upon You and know with confidence that You will look after my life with love and care.

treasure tip
Psalm Day

Written thousands of years ago is the book of Psalms. It is a place in the Bible where I have found strength, solace, and the answer to my prayers in some of my most difficult and discouraging times. Yet it is also a book where I regularly go before I begin my devotion time with God.

If you haven't yet done it, why not write your own psalm or book of psalms to God? You don't have to write as many as King David did, and they don't even have to be as articulate, but it's important that they reflect your heart.

- Start by getting away to a quiet place (your bedroom, a park, anywhere you won't be disturbed).

- Reflect on God and what He's done in your life—His creation, His awesomeness, His faithfulness, and His holiness.

- Go to the book of Psalms in the Bible and select one of your favorite psalms. Go through it and, in your own words, rewrite selected verses or all of it.

- Now try your hand at writing your own psalm to God. Remember God knows your heart, so pour it out to Him in words and verses. It's important to be honest and heartfelt!

It's surprising when we put our hearts and minds to it what we're capable of doing. Before I wrote my own psalms, I used to think that I could never express what I felt the way David did. However, when I started, it was amazing to see how the feelings I had for God deep down just poured out onto the paper.

I loved the experience, and I hope you will too.

ngue. She speaks with wisdom, and faithful instruction is
r tongue. She speaks with wisdom, and faithful instruction
her tongue. She speaks with wisdom, and faithful instructic
on her tongue. She speaks with wisdom, and faithf
struction is on her tongue. She speaks with wisdom, ar
thful instruction is on her tongue. She speaks with wisdor
d faithful instruction is on her tongue. She speaks wi
sdom, and faithful instruction is on her tongue. She speak
th wisdom, and faithful instruction is on her tongue. Sh
eaks with wisdom, and faithful instruction is on her tongu
e speaks with wisdom, and faithful instruction is on h
ngue. She speaks with wisdom, and faithful instruction is
r tongue. She speaks with wisdom, and faithful instruction
her tongue. She speaks with wisdom, and faithful instructic
on her tongue. She speaks with wisdom, and faithf
struction is on her tongue. She speaks with wisdom, ar
thful instruction is on her tongue. She speaks with wisdom
d faithful instruction is on her tongue. She speaks wi
sdom, and faithful instruction is on her tongue. She speak
th wisdom, and faithful instruction is on her tongue. Sh
eaks with wisdom, and faithful instruction is on her tongu
e speaks with wisdom, and faithful instruction is on h
ngue. She speaks with wisdom, and faithful instruction is
r tongue. She speaks with wisdom, and faithful instruction
her tongue. She speaks with wisdom, and faithful instructic
on her tongue. She speaks with wisdom, and faithf
struction is on her tongue. She speaks with wisdom, an

chapter 15:
tame that tongue!

"'Cry-baby,' mocked Blinky."

THE COMPLETE ADVENTURES OF BLINKY BILL (BY DOROTHY WALL)

Proverbs 31:26

"She speaks with wisdom, and faithful instruction is on her tongue."

I recently took my little boy to the zoo for the first time. It was incredibly exhausting and exciting.

We saw the birdeees, snakeees, crocodileees, and woof-woofs. Actually they were lions, but to him they were woof-woofs (or dogeees). Thankfully, these huge, powerfully built cats were behind equally huge, powerfully built enclosures. But they still sent shivers up my spine at their enormity and wildness.

It's strange to think, but we actually have a wild beast also residing inside of us (and no, it's not your hormones). This beast is definitely not as huge as a wildcat but its potential to destroy, harm, and hurt is gi-normous. It's called THE TONGUE!

James 3:7–10 says, *"This is scary: You can tame a tiger, but you can't tame a tongue—it's never been done. The tongue runs wild, a wanton killer. With our tongues we bless God our Father; with the same tongues we curse the very men and women he made in his image. Curses and blessings out of the same mouth!"* (MESSAGE).

The Bible also tells us in Proverbs 18:21 that "life and death exist in the power of the tongue." Incredible, isn't it? We are able to exert life or death through that little pink thing in our mouths. The words we speak have remarkable power to hearten or discourage the people around us.

So let me ask you a question: What words do you speak to the people in your world? Are you like the 31 girl who speaks with wisdom and faithful advice, or do your words literally cut people down with their negativity, cynicism, and criticism?

The old saying, "Sticks and stones may break my bones but names will never hurt me," was definitely penned by one very deluded and rhino-skinned individual. The truth is, words have the power to build us up or tear us down.

The tongue needs to be tamed and controlled in our lives. So let's take our cue from the 31 girl:

Immunize against Foot-in-Mouth Disease
Many people speak before they think, and from their mouth comes toxic gunk that needs a radioactive warning stamped on it. Proverbs 15:28 TLB says, *"A good man thinks before he speaks; the evil man pours out his evil words without a thought."* Once we've spoken, it's impossible to put those words back into our mouths again. Sometimes those words are simply foolish and silly. But sometimes they will cause incredible damage that results in broken friendships and critically wounded hearts.

If you find yourself speaking before thinking then you've developed a habit in your life that needs to be rewired. You can replace this habit with the habit of pausing before speaking and speaking only good things.

Remember, every time you **open your mouth** to talk, your **mind walks** out and **parades** up and down the **words.**
(EDWIN H. STUART)

Jen's Story

My family has never been dysfunctional and never will be. My parents are still madly in love with each other, and my sisters and I are close. Yet I wanted to be like everyone else. I used to lie in bed and hope my parents would have a fight and break up so then I could have heaps of problems, and when I was older, a guy would come and rescue me!

During my elementary school life, I learned to put on masks. I learned that if you were "cool," then you would immediately be liked. So I depended upon the audience to determine who I would be. I said the things I thought other people wanted to hear and became someone else. An impersonator.

In high school I went for a five-week holiday in Brisbane and stayed with my cousins. There I did a lot of soul-searching. In Queensland I realized that I had created so many masks in my life that I no longer knew who I was and decided to discover the real me.

In Brisbane I struggled to know what I thought I liked and who I thought I was. It was in Brisbane that I decided to do something radical and shave my head. It was supposed to be a surprise for when I got home, but my aunt rang home in tears and told my parents. My dad thought I was pregnant! When I came home, my older sister Nyssa cried! It was pretty funny because people treat you different with a shaved head.

When I got home, I came back to God because I realized that who I tried to be in Queensland was someone I chose because she was different. There were a lot of things I thought I liked, but I only liked them because they were different. Instead of deciding whether or not to like something based upon whether it was weird or unusual, I decided I would like what I liked. That might sound weird, but it was a conscious decision I had to make. Otherwise I would end up living the rest of my life as an impersonator of the real me.

At school I had often let people call me bad names. I would joke along with them and even called myself stupid names just to make them laugh. One day I thought about what I wanted in life, and the one thing I most wanted was respect. I got sick of people calling me names because even though I laughed along, they wounded me every time. When I couldn't put up with it any longer, I started standing up for myself and telling people off for calling me names. I didn't let anyone say anything bad about my family or me anymore. Since then my self-esteem has greatly improved.

I guess in my life I have discovered that whatever I deposit in my heart will come out of my mouth. When I started to like and even love who God had made me to be, words of confidence and truth flowed out of my mouth. The more I deposited God's truth in my heart instead of the opinions of others, the more satisfied and happy I was to just be me. The more I planted God's words of life and destiny in my heart, the more masks were unpeeled from my life.

I have discovered that life and death really do flow from our hearts and out of our mouths, creating the worlds we individually live in. And at the end of the day, it's always my choice what goes into my heart and out of my mouth.

Speak Wisely

The book of Proverbs is a book of wisdom, and one of the most practical ways to develop wisdom in your life is to read a chapter of this book every day. There are thirty-one chapters in the book of Proverbs, one for every day of the month. Earnestly seek and desire wisdom in your life. Allow it to deposit in your heart and flow out of your life.

Give Faithful Advice

There will be times in your life when you need to speak truth to a friend that may be hard for them to take. The key is to speak truth "sweetened" with love. Check your heart and motives when it comes time to do this because you may be "artificially sweetening" your truth with a patronizing tone or speaking in a judgemental manner. Real love genuinely cares for the other person's well being. Make sure your heart is pure in its motives when giving advice.

My desire is that we are a generation of girls who speaks with wisdom and faithful instruction. This will take time and self-control, but it is possible to tame our beastly tongues and speak life into our worlds.

Let's Pray

Father,
I desire to be a girl of wisdom and faithful instruction. As I spend time in Your Word every day, I pray that You illuminate it for me and that I can be filled with Your goodness and love.

treasure tip

Tame Your Senses

After all that hard work taming the little beast, it's time again to feel soothed, and there's nothing like aromatherapy oils to do the trick. As mentioned in Chapter 12's Treasure Tip, one of the best ways to enjoy the benefits of aromatherapy is in the bath. In fact, there are few things an aromatherapy bath can't fix. Here are some bath recipes to enjoy:

Detox Bath (for when you've been eating too many McDonald's burgers)
Add two drops each of juniper, grapefruit, and orange oils, or for serious detoxification, dissolve two pounds of Epsom salts. An Epsom salt bath should never be taken more than once a week.

De-Stress Bath (for those times when you just want to scream and pull your hair out)
Add two drops each of lavender, bergamot, and sandalwood oils.

PMS Bath (we all need one of these at least once a month)
Add two drops each of Roman chamomile, geranium, and clary sage oils.

Cold-Banishing Bath (to banish the sniffles)
Add two drops each of eucalyptus, lemon, and frankincense oils.

Muscle-Soothing Bath (after a hard day's work)
Add two drops of lemongrass, lavender, and rosemary oils.

The Good Night's Sleep Bath (for all the insomniacs)
Add two drops each of marjoram, lavender, and mandarin oils.

Energy-Boost Bath (when you're just not firing on all cylinders)
Add two drops each of lime, orange, and lemongrass oils.

Enjoy!

She watches over the affairs of her household and does not eat the bread of idleness.

31 Beauty

chapter 16:
taking things personally

"From then on, Wendy took charge of the Lost Boys in their underground home. They ate well, went to bed early, and Wendy told them lots of stories."

PETER PAN (BY J. M. BARRIE, RETOLD BY VAN GOOL)

Proverbs 31:27

"She watches over the affairs of her household and does not eat the bread of idleness."

I read an article in the newspaper the other day that left me thinking, **"What on earth is the world coming to?"**

It was about a young guy who decided to spray graffiti on a moving train. Of course anyone will tell you that attempting to vandalize a high-powered speeding object is a recipe for disaster. Obviously no one informed this young man. Consequently, he was injured by the train. But instead of accepting that this was a result of his own stupidity, he decided to sue the train company for personal injury—and was successful!

The article was not only highlighting the idiocy of this young man (and others) but also reporting the spiraling costs of insurance and how it is becoming unaffordable; people are suing for damages that are essentially their own faults.

There are many other cases like this one where I shake my head in incredulous disbelief. We are experiencing an outbreak of "victimitis" where people don't want to take responsibility for their actions, and blaming anyone or anything else seems the norm. It's an epidemic known as "passing the buck" and "anything bad that happens to me is your fault." It's an unwillingness to accept personal responsibility.

However, in the life of the 31 girl, we find a very different case. The Bible makes it clear that she keeps watch over her household. The word *watch* means a number of things, but essentially this Scripture reveals that she's the type of girl who is willing to be "vigilant," "take heed," "to guard," and "to take personal responsibility" for her life—her choices, her actions, and her words.

In a world that shirks and shrugs off personal responsibility, this girl thrives on it and, incredibly, not just for herself but for her family too. She is absolutely amazing!

But getting to a place where you accept personal responsibility and blame doesn't happen overnight. It takes time to cultivate an attitude that is open and accepting rather than closed and defensive. An attitude that accepts blame rather than passes the buck.

Here are a couple of tips for you that will help you on your quest to accept responsibility like the 31 girl:

Tip 1: Don't Get Defensive
Being defensive hardens and closes your heart because you don't want to open up and accept that a situation could be your fault. Defensiveness is a sign of a poor self-image because we don't want people to see that we can actually be at fault, and we never want to be the cause of a problem.

Blaming others is as old as time itself. It wasn't Adam's fault that he ate the fruit because that silly Eve made him do it. And it wasn't Eve's fault that she ate the fruit because that sly serpent made her do it. Aaaahhhhhh!!!! Can you see how exasperating being defensive is to other people? Learn to accept that you can be at fault.

Tip 2: Learn to Say Sorry
One of the hardest things to say is "I'm sorry." Learning to say sorry and meaning it is taking a step toward responsibility and accepting blame. You will be surprised how this simple statement can soften the hardest hearts and diffuse the most volatile situations. However, many people refuse to say it because it means that (shock, horror) they were WRONG! Yes girls, I know it's hard to believe but there are times in your life when you will be wrong. And the sooner you learn you are not always right, the sooner your pride can be squelched and humility allowed to wash over your heart.

Any fool can **try to defend** his or her mistakes—and most fools do—but it raises one above the herd and gives one a feeling of **nobility** and **exultation** to **admit** one's mistakes.

(DALE CARNEGIE)

Keera's Story

I was bought up in a single-parent home with my older and younger sister. We were Mom's little girls. My mother struggled to make ends meet from week to week, and we were strongly dependent on her because we didn't have any close relatives.

One day my mom got a new boyfriend, which wasn't unusual, except when I realized that she was pregnant and they were thinking of marriage. I went through the "No, I don't want you to get married. He's going to take you away from us" routine. However, after a little time, I managed to accept the fact. My mom always had a new boyfriend, so I wasn't expecting this to last long. Well, they did marry and ended up having a baby boy.

Darren, her new husband, loved and accepted me as his own. It was almost like we had never been without a father. My stepdad was a truck driver who worked the Perth to Melbourne route; he was away four to six days at a time. Unfortunately, after four years of marriage, they divorced, placing financial pressure on my mom again. They went through a very messy divorce full of accusations of lying and cheating. Because of the stress she was under, my mom gave full custody of my little brother to my stepfather. In one heart-wrenching month, I had lost the only father figure I had ever known and my little brother.

For a long time, my mom went from boyfriend to boyfriend and drug to drug. I went through elementary school doing my own thing without any rules and regulations. The only thing I had to do was check with her if it was okay for me to have sex or take drugs. Basically, she wanted me to do it at home so I wouldn't get injured in the outside world.

For some reason, I never took her up on any of those offers, and I have my friends to thank because without them, I could have ended up a teenage, drug-dependent mom. Every now and then I'd see my little brother Michael, and as time went on, we became closer.

In 1997, when I was in eighth grade, my mother found a new boyfriend, but he was an abusive man whose day job was selling drugs. I was old enough now to know what was going on but was powerless to stop us moving out of my home to go into hiding from people involved in gangs looking for my mother's boyfriend.

My mother again lost all interest in her children's welfare for the man who showed her a little interest (even if he was using her), leaving me to attend to household responsibilities such as cooking, cleaning, washing, shopping, and getting myself and younger sister to school.

Feeling powerless, depressed, rejected, and under pressure, I tried to gain control of my life by moving out of my home to live with my best friend. I moved in and out of my home over a period of seven months. I contemplated suicide, but the thought of leaving my brother and sister prevented me from ever trying. I couldn't leave them to face life on their own. This time of my life was the absolute worst it has ever been. It was a constant struggle to get out of bed and go to school. I was an emotional wreck and pushed my friends away to stop them from ever finding out what was going on.

Finally, after incidents with my mom's boyfriend that involved abuse, violence, police raids, and drug busts, I decided to move out again, but this time taking my sister and mom with me. I checked the newspaper and found a little two bedroom apartment. It was great. I forced my mom to sign the lease papers, and I began packing all our belongings and moving out. When a few days had passed and we were settled, I filed a restraining order against my mother's boyfriend. My mother fought with me, pleading to drop the charges and threatening to leave my sister and me. However, after a major incident of my mother nearly being run over by a vehicle, she decided to stop the relationship, and things started to settle down. She started to take control of her life, leaving me to take control of my own.

Throughout all of this I have witnessed domestic violence and learned how to look after myself, take responsibility for others, take out a restraining order, and defend myself in court. Things a girl of my age should never have to do, hear, or see.

About five months after all of this, in October 1998, I overheard a friend from school talk about a youth rally that was being held at Riverview Church. I went along and gave my broken, lost heart to Jesus. Since then I haven't looked back.

Although I don't have a close relationship with my mom, my family at Riverview has helped me to live life with hope and acceptance of a better, brighter future. I am still working through issues and probably will for the rest of my life, but I am determined not to be a victim of my circumstances. I want my life to be a testament to His saving grace and all-consuming love.

So let's be a different generation and desire to be girls that are softhearted, open, humble, and accepting of our own shortcomings. Rather than being infected by victimitis, let's be girls who take personal responsibility for our actions and lives.

Let's Pray

Father,
I desire to be a girl who is softhearted and open. Help me be teachable, humble, and not get defensive or offended when I am confronted with my faults and weaknesses. I want to grow in Your grace.

treasure tip
girlzONLY girlzNITE

Taking responsibility is important in your personal development. So why not surprise your friends and be responsible for organizing a totally cool girlzONLY girlzNITE? It's also a great way to let your hair down and totally chill out.

Here's the lowdown on what's essential:

- A few of your closest and dearest friends (fifty or so...only kidding)!
- An authentic chick-flick video (*The Princess Bride* is my all-time fave).
- "Chocolate Overload" theme (e.g., hot chocolate and marshmallows, chocolate ice cream and hot fudge topping, chocolate cookies, and anything else chocolate that you can think of).
- Well-worn pajamas or sweatpants (comfort, not glamor, is the key).
- Selection of do-it-yourself pamper products. Giving each other facials, manicures, and pedicures is all part of the package.
- Comfy pillows, blankets, sleeping bags, and countless cushions.
- Really, really yummy, breakfast stuff (e.g. chocolate chip pancakes, chocolate poptarts, chocolate milk, and our favorite...Coco Pops). Are you getting the picture that I love chocolate?

A girlzONLY girlzNITE is all about laughter (lots and lots of girly giggling), love (it's important to develop close friendships), lavishing (totally spoiling each other), and little sleep (you can sleep when you get home)!

e praises her: "Many women do noble things, but you surpa
em all." Her children arise and call her blessed; her husba
so, and he praises her: "Many women do noble things, b
ou surpass them all." Her children arise and call her blesse
er husband also, and he praises her: "Many women do nob
ings, but you surpass them all." Her children arise and call h
essed; her husband also, and he praises her: "Many wom
o noble things, but you surpass them all." Her children ari
nd call her blessed; her husband also, and he praises he
Many women do noble things, but you surpass them all." H
ildren arise and call her blessed; her husband also, and h
raises her: "Many women do noble things, but you surpa
em all." Her children arise and call her blessed; her husba
so, and he praises her: "Many women do noble things, b
ou surpass them all." Her children arise and call her blesse
er husband also, and he praises her: "Many women do nob
ings, but you surpass them all." Her children arise and call h
essed; her husband also, and he praises her: "Many wom
o noble things, but you surpass them all." Her children ari
nd call her blessed; her husband also, and he praises he
Many women do noble things, but you surpass them all." H
ildren arise and call her blessed; her husband also, and h
raises her: "Many women do noble things, but you surpa
em all." Her children arise and call her blessed; her husba
so, and he praises her: "Many women do noble things, b
ou surpass them all." Her children arise and call her blesse
er husband also, and he praises her: "Many women do nob

chapter 17:
don't blow your own trumpet

"Toad got so puffed up with conceit that he made up a song as he walked in praise of himself, and sang it at the top of his voice, though there was no one to hear it but him."

THE WIND IN THE WILLOWS (BY KENNETH GRAHAME)

Proverbs 31:28-29

"Her children arise and call her blessed; her husband also, and he praises her: 'Many women do noble things, but you surpass them all.'"

The Bible is full of some pretty remarkable girls.

There's the orphan girl Esther, who won a beauty contest and consequently became queen of her nation. But that was only the beginning. She ended up risking her life and saved the entire Jewish race from annihilation.

We also have the story of Abigail (1 Samuel 25:18–31), an amazing girl with beauty and brains. In a nutshell, Abigail was unfortunately married to a total numbskull called Nabal. When King David rounded up his men and set off to murder Nabal for his terrible behavior, instead of sitting back and doing nothing, Abigail quickly used her ingenuity and pleaded with David to forgive her husband. She also risked her life like Esther, and because of her gutsy attitude, she changed her destiny forever.

Then there's the story of Ruth. (If you want to read a good love story, forget the ones with Fabio on the cover and instead read the book of Ruth. I always need a box of Kleenex nearby because it has such a romantic ending.) Here was a girl who displayed incredible faithfulness and loyalty and ended up being showered with love and favor (and she found herself a great husband too)!

I could go on and on. In fact, this entire book could be filled with story after story about God's incredible girls. But it's the 31 girl we want to learn from because she is described as outclassing them all.

Proverbs 31:29 makes an amazing statement, *"Many women do noble things, but you surpass them all."*

This girl was world-class, and her family literally raved about her! They sang her praises, enthusiastically gushed, and gave her a standing ovation. And I think that's a key for all of us. Allow others to praise you, and don't blow your own trumpet.

You see Proverbs 31 gives us no indication that the 31 girl sang her own praises. Instead she was content to leave that to others. Proverbs 27:2 says, *"Let another praise you, and not your own mouth; someone else, and not your own lips."* Rather than being egotistical she is a girl of meekness and modesty, which in turn adds to her enchanting appeal.

So, here are two keys to help you avoid becoming a self-taught bugle blower:

1. Eliminate Ego

J. Oswald Sanders said, *"Egotism is one of the repulsive manifestations of pride. It is the practice of thinking and speaking much of oneself, the habit of magnifying one's attainments or importance."*

Egotism is a vile disease and results from being infected by pride. God detests pride because it is a sin where we put ourselves on the throne of our hearts rather than God. Instead of idolizing Him, we idolize ourselves. We become impatient in telling others how important and talented we are. We blah, blah, blah about the awards we've received, the opportunities we've had, the results we've accomplished, and basically how wondrously wonderful we are. We become self-conceited, self-important, and self-opinionated demi-gods, causing those around us to be nauseated by the foul stench of pride.

The good news is that you don't need to go around smelling like a stinky swamp. Ego can be eliminated by its number one enemy—humility. The only way you can kill the odor of pride is to release the scent of humility. And that brings me to my second key:

2. Practice Humility

Humility is a sweet-smelling fragrance that actually draws people to you. It's an attractive quality that catches people's hearts, praises, and compliments.

However, it's important to note that humility is not weakness or spinelessness. Humble people are definitely not doormats. Humility is an *"attitude of personal modesty"* [9] and to practice humility we need to consciously resist the urge to self-promote and self-exalt.

Luke 18:14 says, *"For everyone who exalts himself will be humbled, and he who humbles himself will be exalted."* The 31 girl has no concern about self-promotion because she knows that God is the one who promotes, not man. Many times we're impatient about telling others about ourselves. We want to look good and for other people to have an exalted opinion of ourselves. However, we need to rest in the fact that it's God who promotes one person and humbles the other. And the time will come when He too will promote us; we've just got to be remain humble, faithful, and secure in Him.

Don't be in a rush to hurry the hand of God. God has all the time in the world, and He's prepared to use it to make you into the humble girl He desires you to be.

In the meantime do as Dan Reiland once said: *"Be more concerned about making others feel good about themselves than you are making them feel good about you."*

If you have any good qualities, believe that other people have better ones. (THOMAS A KEMPIS)

real life

Jane's Story (Not the author's real name)

I was born into a Christian family, which I am so grateful for. This doesn't mean that life has been a breeze. I have a mom and dad and two brothers.

My earliest memories that I have are from elementary school. I started first grade in a Christian school where I was the victim of bullies. This continued and I became very clingy to my mom. When we went to church on Sunday, I would cry when I was left at children's church. At school, if I knew my mom was around, I would become physically sick so I could be with her. From an early age my body learned to respond to anxiety by cramping up and resulting in stomachaches so bad that I'd end up in tears.

It wasn't until I was about to finish second grade that my mom finally found out what was going on. At the beginning of the following year, she moved me to the local elementary school, but the damage had already started. I became introverted, making friends with one or two select girls in my class, and at church I tended to keep to myself. I guess I had a false perception of Christians and didn't want to put myself in a situation where I could be bullied again.

In 1988 we were about to move to Brisbane when my doctors said I needed surgery. I was born with a hole in my heart, and now they chose to correct it. So I had surgery. I spent a week in the hospital. I recovered well from the operation, and now my scar is a part of my story.

My memories from my childhood aren't pleasant ones. I was abused at the age of eight by a trusted relative. My world was shattered, and I was the only one who knew. I was too scared to say anything and kept this a secret for the next four years.

216

In the meantime, I started learning to play the classical guitar. Don't ask me why. I think I had the opportunity and took it because my big brother did. I wasn't as good as him, and that was fine with me. The problem was my parents compared me to him, and I started seeing this as a challenge, not something to do because I enjoyed it.

It was at this time that another relative started showing an interest in me. He loved music and everything about music. I still remember that first time he put his hand on my leg. I have something like a photograph of it in my head. I was ten at this time. The abuse carried on for five years. I started to resent the fact that I ever started playing the guitar.

I'd always gone to church. It was part of my weekly routine. Church started to be an escape from my life. I didn't come because I wanted to; I came because I didn't want to spend another second at home. When I came to church, I often felt like going forward for prayer, but my family was there, and I didn't want them asking me questions about my life.

Through this time, I felt totally alone. I was depressed through all my high school life. I became more introverted, and any male was seen as a threat to me. The funny thing is, I joined the school band. I eventually wanted to quit everything to do with music, but my teacher wouldn't let me. I guess at heart I still loved music, I just didn't like what my relative had done to it.

When I was fifteen, I made the most significant decision in my life. My relative had come over while no one was in the house. He actually asked me to run away with him. He wanted me to leave everything behind and leave, right there and then. I actually surprised myself when I firmly told him to leave the house. For the first time in my life that I remember, I was the one who got what I wanted. That was the day I ran into God's arms. I didn't know if God could really do anything for me, even though I was brought up with a knowledge of Him. All I knew was anything was better than what I had at the time.

I met Mary and came to Riverview in 1999. Things were tough, and I just needed to talk to someone. I began to love coming to youth group and felt that for the first time in my life I had finally found Christians who were genuine, who cared, and who were real. I kept coming back, week after week after week.

By 2000, I found myself in leadership at youth group. I'd allowed God to start a mighty work of healing in my life. I was coming out of my shell, stepping out of my comfort zones. I was given the opportunity to speak into the lives of teenage girls and to just love them. I couldn't believe this because, back in 1996, I got a sense that my life would involve ministering to teenage girls.

Over the years, God has continued to heal my heart and is still doing so. I've learned that my abusers don't represent every male on this planet. I'm learning to trust people and that is changing my world dramatically. I no longer hate my life. I love it—the good days, the bad days, and even the days I don't want to face.

I know God has been there with me through everything. He's my comforter, my refuge, and my everything. I have a fair idea where I'd be if I didn't have Him in my life. I'm so blessed that He loved me so much to send His Son to save me. I know that just because things go wrong in my life, it doesn't mean that God intended it to be that way. All that matters to me is that He's the one picking up the pieces of my heart, He's cleaning the gunk out of it and putting it back together. God is truly the restorer of my soul.

Let's Pray

Father,
I want to be a girl who walks humbly before You. May my heart be modest and meek, and may I rest secure and sure in You.

treasure tip
Be a Gem Collector

I love collecting and reading quotes because they challenge, inspire, encourage, and teach me. Why not start a quote collection yourself and allow the words of others to complement your life?

Here's one of my favorite gems, by Ralph Waldo Emerson.

How do you measure success?
To laugh often and much;
To win the respect of intelligent people
and the affection of children;
To earn the appreciation of honest critics
and endure the betrayal of false friends;
To appreciate beauty;
To find the best in others;
To leave the world a bit better
whether by a healthy child,
a redeemed social condition,
or a job well done;
To know even one other life has breathed
because you have lived—
this is to have succeeded.

ars the LORD is to be praised. Give her the reward she ha
rned, and let her works bring her praise at the city gate. Char
deceptive, and beauty is fleeting; but a woman who fears th
RD is to be praised. Give her the reward she has earned, ar
her works bring her praise at the city gate. Charm is deceptiv
nd beauty is fleeting; but a woman who fears the LORD is to b
aised. Give her the reward she has earned, and let her work
ing her praise at the city gate. Charm is deceptive, and beau
fleeting; but a woman who fears the LORD is to be praised. Giv
er the reward she has earned, and let her works bring her prais
the city gate. Charm is deceptive, and beauty is fleeting; but
oman who fears the LORD is to be praised. Give her the rewa
he has earned, and let her works bring her praise at the ci
ate. Charm is deceptive, and beauty is fleeting; but a woma
ho fears the LORD is to be praised. Give her the reward she ha
rned, and let her works bring her praise at the city gate. Char
deceptive, and beauty is fleeting; but a woman who fears th
RD is to be praised. Give her the reward she has earned, ar
her works bring her praise at the city gate. Charm is deceptiv
nd beauty is fleeting; but a woman who fears the LORD is to b
aised. Give her the reward she has earned, and let her work
ing her praise at the city gate. Charm is deceptive, and beau
fleeting; but a woman who fears the LORD is to be praised. Giv
er the reward she has earned, and let her works bring her prais
the city gate. Charm is deceptive, and beauty is fleeting; but
oman who fears the LORD is to be praised. Give her the rewa
he has earned, and let her works bring her praise at the ci

beauty

31

chapter 18:
drop-dead gorgeous

"'How lovely she is!' exclaimed Prince Charming."

SNOW WHITE AND THE SEVEN DWARFS
(FOLKLORE ADAPTED BY WALT DISNEY)

Proverbs 31:30-31

"Charm is deceptive, and beauty is fleeting; but a woman who fears the LORD is to be praised. Give her the reward she has earned, and let her works bring her praise at the city gate."

Our world places a high premium on the outward appearance.

People are lining up to be buffed, bronzed, implanted, polished, pumped, refined, tightened, smoothed, and waxed...and that's just the guys!

The fashion, cosmetics, and gym industries are multi-billion dollar corporations. People are willing to spend big bucks and undergo painful operations in the hope of achieving the body beautiful (plus of course adoration, attention, and fulfillment). They want to halt the aging process through drinking anti-aging elixirs and attending Botox-injecting parties. It seems no one wants to grow old gracefully and fearlessly.

However, 1 Samuel 16:7 says, *"The LORD does not look at the things man looks at. Man looks at the outward appearance, but the LORD looks at the heart."*

It seems safe to say that man and God are at opposite ends of the spectrum when it comes to appearance. What man finds important, God finds insignificant. What man thinks is the secret to happiness, God knows is the answer to misery.

But the secret of true beauty lies not in collagen or Botox but in the Bible. Proverbs 31 starts off with the wise sayings that King Lemuel's mother gave him, the most famous being the description of the 31 girl. And the final verses in Proverbs 31 give us a clue to her enviable life; she was drop-dead gorgeous...on the inside!

Psalm 111:10 says, *"The fear of the LORD is the beginning of wisdom; all who follow his precepts have good understanding."* Here is a girl who has discovered what true beauty is essentially about. She lived her life in fearful, reverential awe of God and knew that outward appearances were secondary to internal beauty.

She knew that her external beauty would not last forever, so it was her heart that she focused upon and desired to fashion after God. And out of her heart flowed love, faithfulness, generosity, compassion, wisdom, grace, and most of all, fear of God. Her lifestyle exuded obedience to God, and as a result, she reaped what she sowed: blessings, praise, and favor from God and man. What an extraordinary girl God has asked us to model ourselves after!

Let's take a look at the foundation for her life:

Fear of God

John Murray said, *"The fear of God is the soul of godliness."*

We are asked to fear God. This doesn't mean in a scared, timid way but with awe and esteem. It's the attitude that elicits from our hearts adoration and love, reverence and honor, focusing upon the majesty, holiness, and glory of God. [10]

Yet, the fear of God seems an old-fashioned concept and it may even be considered embarrassing if you are depicted as a "God-fearing girl." However, being described as God-fearing is undoubtedly the greatest compliment you can hope to receive. It means that you have decided to delight yourself wholeheartedly in all His ways. As S. Maxwell Coder said, *"To do everything the way He would like to have it done and for Him."*

The book *The Practice of Godliness* lists three essential ingredients by the Reverend Albert N. Martin that are needed to develop a fear of God:[11]

1. Know His Nature
C. S. Lewis said, *"We want, in fact, not so much a Father in heaven as a grandfather in heaven—a senile benevolence who, as they say, 'likes to see young people enjoying themselves' and whose plan for the universe was simply that it might be truly said at the end of each day, 'a good time was had by all.'"*

Although God is our heavenly Father who loves and cherishes us, He is also the Creator and King of the universe who is infinitely holy and absolutely hates sin. But because we like to focus more on God's loving nature, we can easily develop a foolishness and familiarity toward Him that is disrespectful. By reading the Bible, you will soon discover that you cannot afford to play games or take God lightly. By discovering His holy nature, you will seek to obey Him, realizing that every sinful act of dishonor and disobedience is an insult to His sovereignty and holiness.

2. Sense His Presence

God is omnipresent, which means that He is everywhere at once and sees all things—our actions, hearts, and thoughts. Nothing escapes Him. By having an awareness of His presence and pervasiveness, we are more inclined to live in awe of Him. However, this is not going to be easy and we can be forgetful of God's presence. But Jeremiah 32:40 says, *"I will inspire them to fear me, so that they will never turn away from me."* God Himself promises to inspire us to fear Him. Why not ask Him to do that for you, and consistently pray for an awareness of His presence and a reverential attitude toward Him.[12]

3. Know His Love

God chose to die rather than live without you! He pursued you, romanced you, and won you over. And it cost Him dearly through the precious blood of Jesus Christ. You owed a debt you could not possibly hope to pay and He paid a debt He didn't owe. God lavishly splurged His love and went to incredible lengths to purchase your salvation. He is the "Hound of Heaven" and is truly an awesome God. So never take for granted the fact that we are able to simply call Him *Father.*.

By grasping this love, your heart will desire to follow Him and live your life forever grateful toward His overwhelming mercy and amazing grace.

I fled Him, down the nights and down the days;
I fled Him, down the arches of the years;
I fled Him, down the labyrinthine ways
Of my own mind; and in the mist of tears
I hid from Him, and under running laughter.
Up vistaed hopes, I sped;
And shot, precipitated,
Adown Titanic glooms of chasmed fears,
From those strong Feet that followed, followed after.
(FRANCIS THOMPSON, *THE HOUND OF HEAVEN*)

Renita's Story

I have always felt God's hand over my life, but it was in 1995 when I made a decision to put Him first that I truly felt His presence. I still remember the night when I decided to put my hand up and follow Him. Although I did not realize it, God started His work in me then. I made a decision to go to a youth camp the next weekend, and it is a time I will never forget. God spoke into me great and scary things. He gave me an insight into what my life might be if I followed Him. Since then God has changed my heart. He's shown me so much of His love that I don't need to search like I used to. I think about how I was prior to God coming into my life. Coming from a broken family and beginning to search for things in the wrong places almost confirms how my life could have turned out.

School was a difficult time. All of my closest friends were such beautiful people—but none of them knew God. Many times at school, when I chose to go against what was termed "normal" by everyone, I felt stupid—like I was missing out on heaps. But God promised that He would never keep any blessing away from me.

Even now my dearest friend is not a Christian—yet—but I know it will happen. I don't know why God doesn't do things straight away. Sometimes I think He wants to hear my heart cry out to Him. I think He wants me to trust Him, so I guess I must do that.

God has blessed me with an inspiring family, loving relationships, success at college, and so much more. It's my prayer that I never take any of it for granted and that I never forget where it came from.

I think, as girls, we want acceptance, success, and love. I also believe we can experience all of this, because if we lay down our lives for God, He will plant a seed of desire in our hearts and show us what He wants us to do. And if we do that, then we will be successful and experience all the blessings that He has planned for us.

When it comes down to it, we're here to worship God. And to me that's standing at the altar and praising Him. It's living my life knowing that it's not mine. It's laying down at night and asking Him for wisdom. And then it's taking that wisdom and speaking it into others' lives. Because that's what it's all about: getting right with God—and then helping others to get right with him too. God bless.

As we come to the end of our adventure of discovering the life of the 31 girl, I hope that you too will fear God—not because you want to be rewarded or praised but because He is the love of your life and your heart's desire is to honor and obey Him.

Proverbs 22:4 says, *"Humility and the fear of the LORD bring wealth and honor and life."* This Scripture is the key to success in the life of the 31 girl. God has exalted her because she fears Him with a humble heart. He generously gives her wealth, honor, and an abundant life.

I hope it is His wisdom that conditions your life and that you seek to beautify your heart through His Word. And my desire is that someday this may also be said of you: *"Many women do noble things, but you surpass them all."*

May you too be internally breathtaking just like the God-fearing 31 girl!

Let's Pray

Father,
I pray that You will inspire my heart to fear You and follow Your ways. I am eternally and overwhelmingly in debt to Your saving love and precious grace. My desire is to grow in internal beauty that is solidly founded on Your Word.

treasure tip
Promise Box

Did you know that the Bible contains as many as 8,000 of God's promises? In difficulty and despair, in temptation, tragedy, trauma, and tiring times of emotional and physical darkness, you can trust these promises. You can be guaranteed without a doubt in the world that God will do for you exactly as He promised.

As we come to the end of this book, I thought it would be good a idea to leave you with one final Treasure Tip that really is priceless—that is, the importance of teaching and reminding yourself of the promises of God and making a **"Promise Box."**[13]

Start by getting yourself a box. You can purchase a boring brown cardboard one from a craft shop and then decorate it yourself, use a shoe box, or buy a nice fancy one from a gift store. Much like a jewelry box, the box itself is not that important; it's what's inside it that counts!

Next up, ask yourself, "What type of promise do I need to be reminded of?" It could be that God loves you or that He will never leave you. Whatever it is, start searching the Bible for promises on that particular topic. Write them down on pieces of paper or cards, and file them away in your precious box.

Here are some examples of God's promises to you:

- **Eternal Life**—*"I give them eternal life"* (John 10:28).
- **Sufficient Grace**—*"My grace is sufficient"* (2 Corinthians 12:9).
- **Strength for Life**—*"I can do all things through Christ who strengthens me"* (Philippians 4:13 NKJV).
- **His Everlasting Presence**—*"The LORD your God is with you wherever you go"* (Joshua 1:9 NKJV).

So open the Scriptures, search for their priceless riches, and treasure their promises. You are royalty, and this is God's inheritance for you.

happily ever after and she lived happily ever after and she lived happily ever after and she lived
happily ever after and she lived happily ever after and she lived happily ever after and she lived
ever after and she lived happily ever after and she lived happily ever after and she lived happily
ever and she lived happily ever after and she lived happily ever after and she lived happily ever
and she lived happily ever after and she lived happily ever after and she lived happily ever after
she lived happily ever after and she lived happily ever after and she lived happily ever after and
lived happily ever after and she lived happily ever after and she lived happily ever after and she
happily ever after and she lived happily ever after and she lived happily ever after and she lived
happily ever after and she lived happily ever after and she lived happily ever after and she lived
ever after and she lived happily ever after and she lived happily ever after and she lived happily
ever after and she lived happily ever after and she lived happily ever after and she lived happily
and she lived happily ever after and she lived happily ever after and she lived happily ever after
she lived happily ever after and she lived happily ever after and she lived happily ever after and
lived happily ever after and she lived happily ever after and she lived happily ever after and
happily ever after and she lived happily ever after and she lived happily ever after and she
happily ever after and she lived happily ever after and she lived happily ever after and she
ever after and she lived happily ever after and she lived happily ever after and she lived happ
ever and she lived happily ever after and she lived happily ever after and she lived happily ev
and she lived happily ever after and she lived happily ever after and she lived happily ever aft
she lived happily ever after and she lived happily ever after and she lived happily ever after an
lived happily ever after and she lived happily ever after and she lived happily ever after an
happily ever after and she lived happily ever after and she lived happily ever after and sl
happily ever after and she lived happily ever after and she lived happily ever after and she live
ever after and she lived happily ever after and she lived happily ever after and she lived happ
ever and she lived happily ever after and she lived happily ever after and she lived happily ev
and she lived happily ever after and she lived happily ever after and she lived happily ever aft
she lived happily ever after and she lived happily ever after and she lived happily ever after an
lived happily ever after and she lived happily ever after and she lived happily ever after and
happily ever after and she lived happily ever after and she lived happily ever after and she
happily ever after and she lived happily ever after and she lived happily ever after and she live

only

epilogue:
and she lived
happily ever after

"The Prince knew then he'd found the girl he loved. They were married and lived happily ever after."

CINDERELLA (FOLKLORE ADAPTED BY WALT DISNEY)

A long time ago, in a land far, far away, there was a beautiful, ancient kingdom.

This exquisite kingdom was ruled by a powerful king and queen, and they had a son named Lemuel.

Prince Lemuel was noble, handsome. and strong. He desired to do what was right and rule his kingdom with wisdom, strength. and integrity. so he would listen to the wise advice of his parents—especially his godly mother.

The queen advised the prince on many things, but the most important words of wisdom she gave him were what to look for in a wife and queen. Prince Lemuel would sit for hours in awe as his mother would describe this beautiful dream girl.

His future bride was painted with so many wonderful qualities that he vowed he would search, even if it took him all his life, until he found a girl like the one his mother had so vividly described.

Little did he know that his mother's advice would later be published in the world's best-seller and be told through the ages to many generations. His "dream girl" would become renowned, celebrated, and legendary...an "ideal" for others to aspire toward. She would be the "It" girl of not only the millennium but for all time.

Well, eventually Prince Lemuel found himself much more than just a girl. She had been hard to find but was definitely worth far more than diamonds, rubies, or any other precious gem.

His princess was exactly as his mother had described. She was loving, faithful, diligent, financially astute, encouraging, disciplined, healthy, positive, compassionate, generous, prudent, stylish, creative, strong, dignified, wise, responsible, and humble. She loved him, but most of all, she feared God.

And as any feel-good story goes, they lived happily ever after.

Endnotes

1. Bingham, D., *"Encouragement: The Oxygen of the Soul,"* Christian Focus Publications, Great Britain, 1997.
2. Poggi, C. A., *Many Thanks for the Things in My Life,* Peter Pauper Press Inc., New York, 1999.
3. Sweeting, G., *Great Quotes and Illustrations,* Word Inc, Texas, 1987.
4. Pipher, M., *Reviving Ophelia,* Random House Inc., New York, 1994.
5. Ibid.
6. Peta Slocombe, counsellor and trainer, Centercare Corporate, Western Australia.
7. Murphy, T., *Programming with Purpose,* Zondervan Publishing House, Michigan, 1997.
8. Osborn, A., *Your Creative Power,* Motorola University Press, Illinois, 1991.
9. Carter, L. & Underwood J., *The Significance Principle,* Broadman & Holman Publishers, Nashville, 1998.
10. Bridges, J., *The Practice of Godliness,* Navpress Publishing Group, Colorado, 1996.
11. Ibid.
12. Bridges, J., *The Joy of Fearing God,* Waterbrook Press, Colorado, 1997.
13. George, E., *Women Who Loved God,* Harvest House Publishers, Oregon, 1999.

girlfriendship
Mary Simpson and Alyson Passauer

Especially for girls in their teens and twenties, *girlfriendship* has been
written by two best friends and features real-life stories, stunning
photography, advice columns, insightful wisdom, and fun tips. This
book will help you recognize the common pitfalls that threaten to
hijack close friendships between girls and, most importantly, how to
avoid them. Ultimately it is about navigating, enjoying, and celebrating
with style this unique ride of life called *girlfriendship*.

ISBN: 0-88368-807-7 • Trade • 224 pages

www.whitakerhouse.com

deepercalling
www.deepercalling.com